Praise for *Money: A Love Story*

*"Stop letting money matters be a source of pain in your life. Read **Money: A Love Story** and allow Kate Northrup to become your new best friend as she guides you, step by step, down the financial freedom trail. Her fresh, creative approach to handling money is sure to leave you feeling empowered and eager to build the wealth you deserve. I loved this book!"*

— **Cheryl Richardson**, author of *The Art of Extreme Self-Care* and *Take Time for Your Life*

*"**Money: A Love Story** is a real breakthrough book! Combining the 'inner game' of money with the 'outer game,' Kate Northrup guides you effortlessly, with humor, compassion, and a deep understanding of what it takes to succeed in life. If you're ready to have a new experience with money and change your financial future, this is the book for you!"*

— **Nick Ortner**, *New York Times* best-selling author of *The Tapping Solution*

"This book guided me to fall madly in love with my relationship to money. Kate Northrup helped me become unapologetic about my desire to earn more, give more, and prosper in every area of my life."

— **Gabrielle Bernstein**, *New York Times* best-selling author of *May Cause Miracles*

"This beautiful book provides the perfect mix of theory and practice. You need your own love story with money, and these pages will lead you to romance."

— **Chris Guillebeau**, *New York Times* best-selling author of *The $100 Startup*

*"This is the first book about finances (and life!) that I can actually relate to. Refreshingly candid, uplifting, and practical, **Money: A Love Story** addresses what holds us back from healing and thriving both personally and financially. I wish I had this book long ago. I can only imagine how much grief I would have spared myself. But as Kate reminds us, it's all part of the spiritual journey to freedom and abundance. Thank you, brilliant Kate Northrup. I am deeply in love with the road map you've given us all."*

— **Kris Carr**, *New York Times* best-selling author of *Crazy Sexy Kitchen*

*"You may know that a healthy relationship with money is essential to attracting abundance and generating financial freedom. What you may not know is that a healthy relationship with your finances is also medicine for a healthy body. With her signature flourish, Kate Northrup teaches us to quit waiting for Prince Charming, take responsibility for our financial well-being, create success on our own terms, lean into feeling-based financial planning, and take actions toward generating revenue without trading hours for dollars. **Money: A Love Story** is just what the doctor ordered for your body, your*

— **Lissa Rankin, M.D.**, *Mind Over Medicine: Sci*

"**Money: A Love Story** is about telling the truth. It's about daring to be courageous enough to just love ourselves where we are—for richer or poorer and without judgment or shame. This book allows us to define what wealth means to us in our own lives and to know our worth no matter what our current circumstances. There is a transformation waiting for all of us in these pages. Kate Northrup offers the financial and emotional wisdom to guide us from a place of lack to a place of abundance with blazing love, raw honesty, and the riveting clarity she has acquired from her own pilgrimage to financial freedom."

— **Meggan Watterson**, author of *Reveal: A Sacred Manual for Getting Spiritually Naked*

"**Money: A Love Story** shows us convincingly that money isn't all about numbers and impersonal charts—it's also deeply emotional, and personal. Kate's section on over-giving to exhaustion vs. giving more value sustainably is worth the price of admission alone, and that is just the beginning. Profound, subtle, and fresh thinking on a topic, which should be as dear to our hearts as it is close to our pockets."

— **Michael Ellsberg**, author of *The Education of Millionaires: Everything You Won't Learn in College About How to Be Successful*

"Kate is presenting us with an intelligent and fun strategy that will bring more abundance and love into the world . . . embrace it and pass it on."

— **Colleen Saidman Yee**, yoga teacher and owner of Yoga Shanti

"Finally, a book to place money and finances in their proper perspective. This is not in praise of or to demonize money but to let it be the tool for supporting the joy of living, a truly modern and yogic view of where the puzzle piece of finance fits with the soul."

— **Rodney Yee**, yoga teacher

"**Money: A Love Story** is a beautiful and insightful guide to finding true prosperity from the inside out."

— **Marie Forleo**, entrepreneur, MarieForleo.com

"Kate Northrup has written a seminal book on money. Building on the past body of knowledge around consciousness and money, Kate has taken the conversation to a whole new level. Having worked with thousands of people around their relationship to money, I know how disempowered most people are and how much suffering is caused by unexamined beliefs in this area of life. I intend to recommend this book not only to all my students, but also to anyone who has not yet found the relationship they want with money. Beware! This practical and powerful book will change your life."

— **Gail Straub**, author and co-founder of the Empowerment Institute

"As an entrepreneur I have had my own very personal journey with money. As someone who works with business owners I watch 99% of my clients struggle with the subconscious relationship that they have with their finances. What I love about Kate's book is that it takes the fear of talking about money away. In an extremely simple and real way you evaluate your relationship, fears, and desires as they relate to money and actually make a plan to be living in the financial reality that you want for life. Love that!"

— **Carissa Reiniger**, CEO and founder of Silver Lining Ltd.

"**Money: A Love Story** gets right to the core of what money is all about: worth. And even more specifically, self-worth. Read this book and learn to not only be smarter about money and have a more loving relationship with it, but also to have a more loving relationship with yourself."

— **Amanda Steinberg**, CEO and founder of DailyWorth.com

MON£Y

A LOVE STORY

MON£Y
A LOVE STORY

Untangle Your Financial Woes
and Create the Life
You Really Want

KATE NORTHRUP

HAY HOUSE

Carlsbad, California • New York City • London
Sydney •Johannesburg • Vancouver • New Delhi

First published and distributed in the United Kingdom by:
Hay House UK Ltd, Astley House, 33 Notting Hill Gate, London W11 3JQ
Tel: +44 (0)20 3675 2450; Fax: +44 (0)20 3675 2451; www.hayhouse.co.uk

Published and distributed in the United States of America by:
Hay House Inc., PO Box 5100, Carlsbad, CA 92018-5100
Tel: (1) 760 431 7695 or (800) 654 5126
Fax: (1) 760 431 6948 or (800) 650 5115; www.hayhouse.com

Published and distributed in Australia by:
Hay House Australia Ltd, 18/36 Ralph St, Alexandria NSW 2015
Tel: (61) 2 9669 4299; Fax: (61) 2 9669 4144; www.hayhouse.com.au

Published and distributed in the Republic of South Africa by:
Hay House SA (Pty) Ltd, PO Box 990, Witkoppen 2068
info@hayhouse.co.za; www.hayhouse.co.za

Published and distributed in India by:
Hay House Publishers India, Muskaan Complex, Plot No.3, B-2,
Vasant Kunj, New Delhi 110 070
Tel: (91) 11 4176 1620; Fax: (91) 11 4176 1630; www.hayhouse.co.in

Distributed in Canada by:
Raincoast Books, 2440 Viking Way, Richmond, B.C. V6V 1N2
Tel: (1) 604 448 7100; Fax: (1) 604 270 7161; www.raincoast.com

A catalogue record for this book is available from the British Library.

ISBN: 978-1-78180-068-3

Printed and bound in Great Britain by TJ International Ltd, Padstow, Cornwall.

*To my man, Mike, for helping
make our whole life a love story.*

CONTENTS

Join the Money Love Community Today!   xiii

Foreword   xv

Introduction   xxi

A Money Love Quiz   xxvii

CHAPTER 1: What's Love Got to Do with It?   1

CHAPTER 2: It's Not about the Money   29

CHAPTER 3: Woo-Woo Meets Cha-Ching   61

CHAPTER 4: You've Got You, Babe   77

CHAPTER 5: What Can You Do to Pay Attention?   103

CHAPTER 6: You Owe You   129

CHAPTER 7: Feel-Good Financial Planning   153

CHAPTER 8: True Financial Freedom   177

Conclusion: But Seriously, What's the Point?   197

Appendix: Financial Freedom Freeways   207

Resources   229

Acknowledgments   231

About the Author   237

JOIN THE MONEY LOVE COMMUNITY TODAY!

This book is only the beginning of your love affair with your money, yourself, and your life. There's a whole lot more fun for you over at www.moneyalovestory.com.

Ongoing support and community are critical for success in any area of your life. One of the biggest factors in my own ongoing financial (and overall) wellness has been a posse of women holding one another accountable, being guides for each other, cheering one another on, and loving one another. I want this for you, too.

I've put together more resources, education, programs, tools, and ongoing support for you. Join me at www.moneyalovestory.com and learn how you can:

1. **Join our exclusive online community.** Connect with other people reading the book and experiencing results. Ask questions. Give answers. Prosper in community.

2. **Start a Money Love Circle.** Download a free guide to starting your own local or

virtual community to take the Money Love journey with.

3. **Do the exercises.** Download PDFs of all the exercises in the book to fill out on your computer or print out.

4. **Download a coaches guide.** Want to incorporate the material in *Money: A Love Story* into your coaching practice? I've created a guide to make it seamless and effective for both you and your clients.

5. **Access exclusive webinars, videos, programs, recommendations, interviews, and articles.** The material in this book is living and breathing in my own life. As I find new material and have fresh insights I'll be sure to share them with you on the site.

6. **Share your success.** Share your own story of falling in love with your money, yourself, and your life. Read other people's stories to keep you inspired.

Visit www.moneyalovestory.com to join in the fun and go deeper with the book.

FOREWORD

Christiane Northrup, M.D., author of
Women's Bodies, Women's Wisdom

How well I remember the day that I first went with Kate's father to meet our stockbroker following Kate's birth. A new baby meant that it was time for some estate planning. I walked into this venerable financial institution (which no longer exists)—newly postpartum, feeling frumpy, fat, and ignorant—holding newborn Kate. Our broker, in sharp contrast to me, was dressed in an impeccably tailored suit with perfect white cuffs and cufflinks—a vision of sartorial splendor. The offices were paneled with expensive walnut or cherry, and they oozed "money." There wasn't a single piece of paper on his desk. Pristine. Perfect. Barren. He spoke almost exclusively to my husband. And the entire conversation was about how much money we needed to put away in order to have a certain income when we retired. The conversation boiled down to this (from my point of view): "Right now, restrict every pleasurable aspect of your life that costs money. Scrimp and save. For the next 30 years. Then—and only then—will you be able to live well once you retire." What I heard was this: "Put life on hold now. Live later." There was nothing in the conversation that made any sense to my soul or to my belief in the abundance of the universe. Nothing about joy or living. Completely devoid of emotion or life force. Moreover I felt judged and unworthy compared to this perfectly dressed individual and his staff. The entire experience was intimidating. If this was finance, I didn't want anything to do with it.

Of course, unbeknownst to me, I was perpetuating my family's financial patterns, following in my father's footsteps. He was an ebullient man who knew how to make money as a dentist, but who, when he suddenly died at the age of 68, left my mother without any substantial financial security. Happily my brothers stepped in and salvaged the situation so that she, literally, got to keep the farm! Looking back now, I see that Kate's father was playing the role of my mother (who always worried about money and taxes) while I was carrying on the legacy of my father, who spent freely without much planning for the future!

But there's another layer to this money story for nearly all of us—and this is the layer that *Money: A Love Story* really addresses. Western culture has long operated under the notion that frugality is a function of morality. The less you spend, the holier you are. And if you desire nice things and a full life, you are not as morally upright as the tightwad. This belief, which stems from the Puritans, is what my father and I were actually reacting against. But there is no power in unconsciously reacting against a belief you don't even realize you have. Your power to create your own love story with money begins with examining—kindly—your own behavior and beliefs about money so that you can transform them.

And so it is with great delight that I now get to enjoy financial literacy—and to witness through my daughter the healing of her financial lineage. Which, of course, is intimately related to my own. I reveled in reading the part of this book that Kate was most nervous about: her family money legacy and our business history together. No worries there, sweetie. You told the whole truth and nothing but the truth—and in a very graceful, elegant, and loving way. Not an easy thing to do about a subject as charged with emotion as money, divorce, and one's parents. Talk about family secrets!! We all have a unique money legacy, of course. And talking openly and freely about money in families is not common. So it takes courage—and the willingness to look at and change your own consciousness about this subject.

Reading this book is kind of like holding my first literary grandchild!!! The first thing I did after reading the introduction was take the Money Love Quiz. My score was very high. Over 30—a testimony to what a *very* long way I have come since the days of financial ignorance that were the soil in which Kate's financial education is rooted. And now, from the ashes of this legacy, a beautiful feminine phoenix has risen!! *Money: A Love Story* brings kindness and compassion to the subject of money. This book is filled with emotion, meaning, and life force. It is filled with what Catherine Ponder calls "radiant Divine Substance"—the energy that is behind all manifested form. The energy that creates worlds. The energy of abundance and joy and plenty—the feminine "things worth living for."

Money: A Love Story is, of course, also filled with absolutely practical hands-on, no-judgment ways to heal your own money legacy. Here's something that I did to clear up my own legacy—and heal that shame imprint I mentioned above without passing it on to my daughters. Right after my divorce and during my fast track to financial literacy, I made sure I took my daughters (then in their late teens) into the very same financial institutions in which I had felt so inadequate. I wanted them to meet my "financial team"—my accountant, my lawyer, my banker, my financial planner. I wanted them to know that people who work in the financial industry are hired by them. To work for them—not the other way around. I didn't want my daughters to feel powerless in the hallowed halls of financial institutions. I wanted them to have an experience of financial support—of having their own individual values honored. I didn't want them to feel judged or stupid or anything else negative when it came to their money And by the way, I let them know (proudly) that I went through three different accountants before I found one who was exactly right for my needs. The first two treated me like a silly girl. Nuts to that!!! I also, of course, fired the broker who was not interested in talking to me when Kate was a baby, but became very eager to meet with me following my divorce and a modicum of financial success.

Here's the whole truth. Our relationship with money profoundly affects our health, particularly the health of the second chakra—our organs of reproduction, the bladder, parts of the bowel, and the low back. For years and years as an ob/gyn physician I have seen up close and personal how a woman's health is affected by issues of money, sex, and power—second chakra energies. For example, a woman's pelvic health is generally good when she has control over her own finances versus being controlled by the finances of others. Or feeling unworthy to accept more money for the work she does. Another health risk for a woman is feeling as though she can't leave an abusive relationship because she can't survive on her own financially. In short, there are a whole host of reasons why *Money: A Love Story* is really a book about health. When you have health in your finances, it's infinitely easier to have health in your body. Full disclosure: I personally developed a large fibroid tumor in my uterus in the last three years of my marriage—a testimony to the fact that my second chakra creative energies were not balanced well back then.

And so, I love that my own daughter, who was brought up knowing the link between beliefs and health, has looked her own money legacy straight in the eye—and then, with love and tenderness, changed the barren parts into an oasis of consciousness and practical wisdom. Through the eyes of my own child, I can see how very far I, too, have come—from financial terror to financial freedom. As a result, my grandchildren—and maybe you and your children or grandchildren—will be spared from the barrenness and fear that have surrounded the subject of money for millennia. And like me and my daughter, you can change your relationship with money into a love story that uplifts not only you, but everyone you touch. And to you, Kate, I say, Well done. Well done. I am so proud of you I could burst.

INTRODUCTION

Anyone who says they don't have money issues is lying—or perhaps they're simply delusional. Money is so omnipresent in our lives and yet so rarely discussed on a deeper level that we don't even understand the influence it has on us.

You see, the thing about money is that it's a stand-in for something else. In essence, we trade money for what we want, for things that, in our eyes, have a certain value. The economy is simply a system of value exchange. That's it. Money in and of itself is nothing. It's what money *represents* that makes the whole shebang a little complex.

For some, money is a stand-in for love. For others, it's a stand-in for comfort or joy or pleasure. And for others, money is a stand-in for happiness. And this assigning of value brings with it all the emotions of any relationship. That, my friends, is why I titled this book *Money: A Love Story.*

I'm sure some reading this title will be appalled that I had the nerve to use *money* and *love* in the same sentence. To even suggest that money is related to love has the power to offend. Yet I'm so sure that unraveling our money woes has everything to do with love (and very little to do with anything else) that I was willing to put it on the cover of this book.

I have yet to meet someone who doesn't have an emotional charge around money. Whether they have millions of dollars or a few singles to their name, money carries some serious weight for nearly every individual living in our culture. However, despite money being such a weighty issue for some, it's not possible to survive anywhere on the vast majority of the planet without participating in the economy in some way. So, it's about time we got our money story straight.

♡

Most people who admit to having money problems think that the way to start the whole process of fixing them is by learning more of the right actions to take around their money. They think that if they were just to read the right personal finance book or invest in the right stocks or hire the right CPA that all would be well. But from what I've found, these folks are approaching it from entirely the wrong direction.

In my experience of moving from debt to financial freedom—and the experiences of others whom I've observed—I've come to realize that the most important place to start is also the one that's most often overlooked: ourselves. Figuring out where we stand with money takes a lot of self-reflection and understanding. Because, as with any good love story, our relationship with money has its ups and downs and twists and turns. We're enamored. We're in love. We hate its guts and swear we will never do "xyz" again. We fight. We make up. We let go too fast and hold on too long.

As with any relationship, the key to dealing with your financial woes lies within. It's not about beating yourself up or putting strict guidelines on what you can and cannot buy. It's about seeing the part you play in your relationship. It's about identifying the value of things in your life. It's about seeing who you truly are in relation to money. To have a good relationship with money, you must know who you are and what your purpose is in this world.

This was made especially clear to me when I was interviewing Danielle LaPorte and her friend Navjit Kandola. At the end of our video (which you can see at www.moneyalovestory.com/glimpse) Navjit asked me a thought-provoking question: What future do you belong to? In essence, she was asking what gets me energized and excited enough to care about life. It was an opportunity to put a true face to my desire to live my life's purpose, and it highlighted for me, once again, that being able to live this life is inextricably linked to money and my relationship with it. And the same is true for everyone. To wake up every morning and do whatever calls to you, whatever the heck you feel like doing, is connected to your ability to feel free from financial strain and be open to what your heart is telling you.

Before we jump into the nitty-gritty talk of money, I want to be very clear that my philosophy is *not* that having more money leads to financial freedom. The great mistake that most people make is that, when they talk about financial freedom or imagine it for themselves, they either don't know what it means or they think it has to do with amassing millions. There are hundreds, most likely thousands, of books out there about how to make more money, preferably *a lot* more money. I've read many of them, and I have gleaned some wonderful wisdom and advice that I've implemented in my own life. In fact, you may recognize some of this advice peppered throughout the pages you hold in your hand.

Let me be clear, though, that this book is not about amassing wealth. This book is about organizing your life so that you have what you truly want. I will walk you through strategies that will help you get more clear about your finances, get out of debt, and be on your way to financial freedom by focusing both on your emotional life and your external financial practices—which are also ultimately connected to your emotional life.

While I don't have a preconceived notion of what your purpose on the planet is, I do know that to live it you must be totally present. And it's much easier to be present when you don't have static in your financial life—static that can hold you back from enjoying expansive, big thinking about the state of the world and what you have to offer, as well as from relishing in the deliciously mundane moments of walking your kid to school or watching a fire burn in your wood stove. When you're present you can hear yourself better. Then you can be of greater service and give your whole self—mind, body, and soul. In *The Fire Starter Sessions* my friend Danielle LaPorte says "Becoming you is your purpose." And the bottom line is, it's easier to become you, the most robust version, when you're not freaked out about money all the time.

Since it's virtually impossible to avoid relating to money in some way, why not make it a linchpin in your approach to life, even incorporating it into your spiritual philosophy and practice? I've done this over the past several years and the results have been miraculous—I went from being $20,000 in debt to having total financial freedom. I've learned a lot on my journey, and

I'm excited to share the tips and techniques that have paved my way.

Remember, your road to a good relationship with money will be unique to you—just like any relationship. While this book is structured to move from an exploration of the internal aspects of your money relationship to the external aspects of how we interact with money on a daily basis, I don't expect that this will match how you come to know yourself in respect to your finances. The exercises you find throughout build on one another and help you gain more insight on yourself, but you may find yourself lingering on one for weeks while you whip through another quickly. Trust your timing and take the time you need. The only advice I will give is that you shouldn't skip any chapters altogether. If you feel resistance, that chapter or exercise may be the one that ends up being the most important for your journey with money.

So take what I've written and give it a shot in your own life. I guarantee that something will change for the better. I can't tell you exactly how or what, but I know positive attention paid to any area of your life yields tremendous results, and I also know from experience that such attention on the financial area of life is well worth it.

One quick note before you begin. The most helpful tool for putting some loving attention on your money is a journal, and many of the exercises in this book will ask you to write out your thoughts and note where your finances stand. So grab a blank journal and designate it your Money Love Journal. Beyond that, all you'll need is a pen and a willing heart and mind. So how about it? Let's get started.

A MONEY LOVE QUIZ

Before you jump into the main part of the book, it's good to establish where you stand now in your relationship to money. Take this quick quiz to learn what's holding you back from the abundance you desire and what your current relationship with money says about you. Plus, find out how you can personally get the most out of this book.

1. Do you know how much you spent last month and on what within about $100?

2. Do you know how much you made last month within about $100?

3. Do you have more than $1,000 in savings?

4. Do you have at least one retirement account?

5. Do you have at least one investment account?

6. Do you have any sources of income that come in no matter if you work or not, such as real estate investments, stocks and bonds, or businesses?

7. Do you know which funds/stocks/bonds you own in any investment accounts that you have?

8. Do you talk about money with your significant other, a friend, or someone else close to you at least once a week?

9. Do you know how much money is in your bank account right now within $100?

10. Do you know how much you spend on average per month?

11. Do you know what top three categories you spend your money on?

12. Do you consciously spend money on the things you most value?

13. Do you enjoy taking financial actions like paying bills, talking to your accountant, and checking in on your investments?

14. Do you enjoy what you do for a living?

15. Have you ever read a book about money before this one?

16. Have you ever taken a course about money?

17. Do you feel optimistic about your financial future?

18. Do you set financial goals at the beginning of each year?

19. Do you track your expenses?

20. Do you feel that the work you do is adding value to the world?

21. Do you like making money?

22. Have you ever started a business?

23. Do you sometimes lie awake in bed at night or wake up early worrying about your finances?

24. Do you believe people who are wealthy are less spiritual than people who have less money?

25. Do financial conversations with your friends or a significant other often end in disagreements?

26. Do you feel anxious when you think or talk about money?

27. Do you find yourself using the phrase "I can't afford that" at least once a week?

28. Do you have credit card debt?

29. Do you avoid looking at bank statements, credit card bills, and other financial paperwork?

30. Do you owe any back taxes?

31. Do you feel like there's never enough when it comes to money?

32. Do you space out, get bored, or exhibit other signs of resistance when learning about money, talking about money, or engaging in your financial life in other ways?

33. Does spending less than you make feel limiting to you?

34. Do you have a belief, even a barely conscious one, that money is bad or dirty?

35. Do you have a belief, even a barely conscious one, that rich people are evil and/or greedy?

36. Do you feel drained by the work that you do for money?

37. Do you have problems spending money on yourself?

38. Do you feel anxious when spending what you consider to be a large sum of money?

39. Do you keep a balance on your credit card despite knowing that you could easily pay it off?

SCORING:

Add up your yeses from questions 1–22. Write that number here ____.

Add up your nos from questions 23–39. Write that number here ____.

Add the first number to the second number. Your total Money Love Score is ____.

If your score is 0–11: You and your money are on the outs. Let's face it: money is not your favorite subject. It's been a rough ride when it comes to your finances. Congratulations, though, for taking the brave step of going through this quiz. The mere act of going through the assessment and being honest about your financial situation takes a lot of courage. Your showing up and starting to get clear on your relationship to money shows willingness. And the first step to transformation is being willing. You're already ahead of the game because, as Woody Allen says, "Eighty percent of success is showing up." You have some work to do to clear out the cobwebs of limiting beliefs in your money consciousness. And there are some practical steps you'll need to take to get your financial house in order. Your relationship with money is tumultuous. It's not been a love affair in the past and you may be scarred. But that can change starting today. The good news is you're here, you have this book in your hands, and you're willing. You're in the perfect place at the perfect time.

How you can get the most out of this book: Easy does it. If you find yourself feeling afraid or overwhelmed, give yourself permission to take a break. Just promise yourself that you'll finish this book and all the exercises in it within a year. Grab a girlfriend (or better yet, a whole gaggle of 'em) and support each other on this journey. Falling deeply in love with your money (and yourself) so that you can have a life that you love is not for the faint of heart. But I promise you that the benefits of abundance, freedom, and truly valuing yourself are worth getting uncomfortable for. This book is more than likely going to make you uncomfortable. When it does, congratulate yourself. Being uncomfortable means you're growing. Your future is bright. Stick with me. We're going through this together.

If your score is 11–30: Love is in the air. I see some canoodling in your future! You are well on your way to being a money maven. Well done, you! You may still have some limiting beliefs to clear out or some debt to pay off, but you're on your way, baby! It's time to turn up the heat and snuggle up even closer to your money. You've already made some fantastic headway but there's still some room to grow. The great thing is, the better it gets, the better it gets. Any relationship worth having is worth deepening by taking regular, loving actions.

How you can get the most out of this book: Read with an open mind and an open heart. The way I talk about money isn't the way most people talk about money. This book combines the spiritual with the financial. This isn't done many other places. If you find yourself getting frazzled by the processes in the book, stay present. You're already on your way to a wonderful, loving relationship with your money. Also, if you feel bored because you already know something, stick with it anyway. Do the exercises even if you feel like you know everything about that topic—it's possible that you may discover something you didn't know you didn't know. Really great relationships require us to go places we've not gone before. Chances are that you and I are going to go some of those places together. Don't worry. I've got your back. This is actually going to be fun.

If your score is 30–39: It's true love! You live in the rarified air of people having a delicious love affair with their money. You understand how money works and you're not afraid to talk about it or engage with it. Relationships take daily investment, however. Anyone who's been married for several years or longer will tell you that it takes work. Make the choice today to stay engaged with your money in a loving way. Don't get complacent. Instead, take daily, loving actions nurturing your relationship with money.

How you can get the most out of this book: Be careful of the I-already-know-this syndrome. When you've already read other books on money, have taken classes, and are already on the abundance train you may fall prey to this insidious syndrome. Any time you find yourself checking out because you think you already know something, it's a great opportunity to reengage. I don't believe there are any 100 percent original ideas out there, but we do need to hear things many, many times before they sink in. You may have heard some of what I've written here. But I promise you this: you have this book in your hands for a reason. We've found one another and there's something here for you. Surrender into the depth of experience that can come from having a beginner's mind. Approach this work as though it's absolutely brand new. We all have the potential to dive deeper into our relationship with our money, with ourselves, and with love itself. This is your opportunity and the time is now. Let's dive in together, shall we?

Chapter 1

WHAT'S LOVE GOT TO DO WITH IT?

To answer the question posed by the fabulous Tina Turner and by the title of this chapter, in a word: *everything.*

Let's begin by looking a little more in depth at the concept I presented in the Introduction, about what money really is . . . or isn't: money doesn't exist. What?! Go back and make sure you read that correctly. Yep, you did.

I'll repeat that. Money doesn't exist. The first recorded use of the term *money* goes back to 3000 B.C. in Mesopotamia. Humans needed a system of exchange to keep track of their valuable things, and so money was born. Essentially, we made it up. The fact that we can say the house I'm writing this in, located in the middle of the desert outside of Scottsdale, Arizona, is worth $500,000 is made up. The fact that it cost me $45 to get a pedicure last week and $39.95 to buy the shorts I'm wearing is all completely dependent on our human perception of value.

The green-and-white rectangles of paper in my wallet are practically worthless in and of themselves. So are the little plastic cards with embossed numbers that I use to pay for stuff. They have no intrinsic value. When you really step back and take a moment to look at the whole money system objectively, you realize that money, in fact, does not exist. Humans made it up.

So, next time you're wailing about the state of the economy and feeling helpless and hopeless about your financial situation, take a moment for a reality check. Open up your wallet and take out the pieces of paper and plastic that are the supposed cause of your woe. Give 'em a good look. Sniff 'em. Touch 'em. Crinkle 'em around or tap 'em against each other and listen to 'em. What are these pieces of paper and plastic actually? They're simply symbols of value that we human beings have created.

YOUR MONEY STORY

Now that we've established that money isn't real, however, we can also acknowledge that we do, indeed, have pretty intense emotions connected to it, and now is a good time to start exploring them. And what better way to begin this process than by looking at our own personal stories with money? The first stage to becoming financially free is to tell the truth of your story to yourself, and feel your feelings around it if you haven't previously done so (or even if you have—generally emotional healing happens in layers and stages). This is important because the truth seeps out eventually, even if you're trying to ignore it. So you might as well invite it out into the light consciously and with love so it doesn't bite you in the ass later, when you least expect it.

My mom has always told me that you have to feel it to heal it. This is one of my life's maxims. I don't think that life is about being happy all the time. I think it's about feeling the entire spectrum of human emotion so that we've lived out every moment to the fullest extent we possibly can. So let's jump right in with my money story, which comes with as many twists and turns as the next girl's.

I do this not so much because I think my story is inherently interesting, but instead to give you the opportunity to see yourself reflected in my journey. As you read my story and those of others throughout this book, notice which ones resonate with you and which ones turn you off. Notice what annoys you and what makes you really excited. Pay attention to where you have a strong emotional reaction, positive or negative. There are golden nuggets of wisdom for you in each of those stories so listen up; my words may be your inner voice manifest in ink on these pages.

I grew up in a Waspy household in Maine with two parents who were doctors. My mom came from a family of above-average income compared to most of the people in her town. My dad came from a family who had inherited money from Alcoa aluminum and grew up with maids and someone who came to polish the silver once a week. Growing up, my sister and I wanted for nothing. We were extremely well provided for, from dance classes to vacations to college tuition.

There was not, however, much discussion of money in our household. In fact, no one really ever talked about it. I remember that once a year, not long after my birthday on the first day of spring, my dad got out a lot of pieces of paper with lines of numbers on them. He would then spread them out on the living room floor in piles, get out his highlighter, and begin to attack. The whole thing looked quite complex and appeared to really stress him out. Nonetheless, it wasn't particularly discussed.

The reason I even knew that my family had a fair amount of money was mostly because of what my friends would say. They would ask me things like, "How does it feel to be rich?" and "How much did that outfit cost? I bet just your shoes cost more than everything I'm wearing put together." I knew that other parents respected (or resented, depending on the person) my parents because they were doctors. I knew we went out to eat a lot. I knew that we took trips and that when it was time to buy new ballet slippers because I'd outgrown the old ones, it didn't seem to be a problem.

I also liked making money from a very early age. My sister, Ann, and I started our first business together when I was about six and she was about eight. It was called Queen Anne's Lace and Katydids. We sold lemonade, bouquets of wildflowers, and handmade jewelry on an island called Chebeague off the coast of Maine in the summers. I then went on to have a booming dog, cat, and babysitting business through my teens. I was also regularly the top salesperson in our class fundraisers, selling the most magazine subscriptions, boxes of oranges, or wreaths depending on the year and the sport I was playing at the time. My success simultaneously embarrassed me and made me proud because of the attention I received for it.

Though my parents didn't talk to my sister and me much about money, I was aware that it was important. I noted that my friends and their parents seemed to put quite an emphasis on it, as well.

My parents got divorced after 24 years of marriage when I was 16. Suddenly there were more conversations around money than ever before. I was now interacting with my parents separately about it for the first time. I got to see how differently they interacted with it and the different philosophies they had around it. That was when my true financial education began because there was so much contrast. I began to pick and choose which perspectives I felt really made sense to me.

During the time after the divorce my mom began her own financial education. She, like many women, had assumed my dad was better with money than her. He was tall, handsome, and a third-generation Harvard graduate who came from money. My mom had received no financial education growing up in the 1950s, and though she was an incredibly successful doctor, she'd never gotten up to speed on finances. She found the whole subject terminally boring so she just opted out. Until, of course, she found herself in the midst of divorce and carrying a great deal more financial responsibility on her shoulders than ever before.

For the first time in her life it occurred to my mom that being good with money was more than simply believing in a "prosperity mind-set." It turns out that when you're afraid you're going to lose your home and you have to go back to the dump to retrieve your old faucet when you realize that the new one costs $250, there's more to taking care of your financial life than doing affirmations—though this can be one piece of a financial stewardship puzzle.

Luckily my mom not only got scared she also got moving. She realized that she was a 50-year-old woman with a *New York Times* best-selling book (*Women's Bodies, Women's Wisdom*) who had been a guest on *Oprah* and had a very successful medical practice, but who knew very little about money. She started reading every money and prosperity book she could get her hands on. For whatever reason, at the ripe young age of 16, I had an insatiable appetite for books on money. So as my mom read Catherine Ponder's *The Dynamic Laws of Prosperity, Think and Grow Rich* by Napoleon Hill, and *Rich Dad, Poor Dad* by Robert Kiyosaki, I read them all right alongside her.

It was around this same time as I watched my mom get totally freaked out about money that I made a vow to myself: I would never end up in that position. I saw how she had willingly given her financial power away. She had made a negative assumption about her ability to handle her finances, and then at the age of 50, she had to dramatically change course. I simply wouldn't let that happen to me.

Another thing that I began to reflect upon at this time was the nature of achievement and how that relates to money. As a child I could sense both my parents really pushing and striving. What was modeled for me was that doingness was next to godliness. I got two related messages: that more hours spent working were better and that financial success was very important. I didn't really know what financial success meant, and it wasn't ever directly discussed, but I got the message loud and clear regardless.

There was definitely a culture of achievement in my family, and my sister and I followed suit, both attending Ivy League universities. I went on to graduate magna cum laude from Brown while at the same time performing in two dance companies, acting, singing, and dancing in musicals, having a thriving social life, and starting a business.

Yet, even though the achievement imprint was strong in me, that didn't mean I hadn't begun to think about how hard my parents worked while I was growing up—even before I went off to college, this was on my mind. During my childhood, both of my parents had had successful medical practices of which they were part owners. Both of them were on call a lot, waking up at 3 A.M. because someone had an emergency or was having a baby. My mom also managed to write a *New York Times* bestseller while practicing medicine. And then there was being parents, which was in no way an afterthought. Despite their busy lives, both of my parents showed up at every parent-teacher meeting, soccer game, and play I ever had.

Though my parents made a lot of money and did manage to make time for the things that meant a lot to them (like my second-grade production of *Goin' Buggy*), they didn't strike me as free. My mom wrote during most weekends and she traveled for speaking engagements frequently. My dad was often either on call or going to the hospital to make his rounds. It seemed as though there was always a pressing work matter to deal with, even though we were able to spend a lot of time as a family. This meant that our time together was often colored by things going on in my parents' careers. Whether they were discussing the surgeries they'd done that day over dinner or swinging by the hospital to do rounds on the way home from being out for breakfast on the weekends, work was always there.

I knew that I liked the kind of experiences that my parents' work could afford us like eating out, seeing shows on Broadway, and traveling. But I also knew on some level, even before I could fully articulate it, that I wanted the freedom to spend my time the way I wanted to spend it. And by the time I was 16, I had recognized that freedom did not mean working harder and harder to earn more and more money as though I had a gun to my head. The seed of my desire for freedom had been planted.

So, in addition to following my mother's example of self-education about money, I set about expanding and deepening my own financial education over the next several years. I read everything in the Robert Kiyosaki Rich Dad series. I created my own prosperity affirmations. I attended seminars about prosperity mind-set. I took every entrepreneurship class offered at Brown. I immersed myself.

In his book *Rich Dad, Poor Dad*, Kiyosaki says that if you want to learn about creating financial freedom and a successful business you should spend five years with a good network marketing company. (A network marketing company is a company that manufactures a product and then uses a word-of-mouth marketing model to spread the word and distribute the product.) At the time that she read this book my mom had been using and recommending the supplements of a company called USANA Health Sciences for years. The supplements happened to be distributed through network marketing. Because of her connection to the brand, she decided to start a USANA distributorship to get more fully into the business—something she'd never considered doing before. I guess the beauty of being scared shitless is that, if you're lucky, you're more open to trying things that you wouldn't have otherwise.

Though my mom felt like network marketing might be a great way to learn about business and create residual income, she was still slightly reticent and decided that it would be a great idea for *me* to do that business. So, she gave me her USANA distributorship, and I began building a network marketing business at the age of 18. There I was calling all my parents' friends and my friends' parents to invite them to slideshow presentations in my mother's living room.

As my mom gave herself a financial education, she began implementing a lot of the strategies she was learning about in her various meanderings in the business, metaphysical, and personal finance worlds, and she began to have some great success. By a divine, angelic spark, Oprah read and loved my mom's books. This contributed to her star rising very quickly.

It was just my mom and me living at home after my parents' divorce because my sister had left for college. And due to my mom's increased success, the financial pendulum swung in the direction of one of her favorite, albeit tongue-in-cheek, sayings, "Nothing succeeds like excess." We went on amazing vacations. We went shopping at high-end boutiques on Newbury Street in Boston. We stayed at beautiful hotels. We ate out all the time.

And the truth is, this was a higher level of opulence than what we'd previously been accustomed to as a family, but the sensation of experiencing abundance in the form of my mother spending money, not necessarily extravagantly, but somewhat freely and particularly on shared experiences like nice meals out, was not new for me. She had always seemed relatively comfortable spending money on the things she valued, generally trusting that there was enough.

Soon, I started college, and the work on my USANA business began to pay off; I was earning weekly income beginning in my freshman year. I had a much-higher-than-average income for a college student. And I translated that directly into much-higher-than-average expenses. Suffice it to say, I probably spent more time during my Brown career at Nordstrom than I did at the John D. Rockefeller library. My parents had always told me that when I got a credit card I must never carry a balance; I must pay it off every month. During school my income was enough to pay for my rent, my books, and my credit card bill without a problem.

Despite my above-average income, though, I didn't manage to amass much in the way of savings. I'll never forget standing in the post office with a friend retrieving one of my USANA checks. I had just gotten the envelope when she asked how much I made. When I told her, she said, "Wow, so you must have quite a bit in savings." I simply smiled, but inside I was cringing. Savings? It was almost as though she'd uttered a word in a foreign language. It had never occurred to me to save my money. Each month I simply spent the same amount I earned, regardless of the fact that my foundational living expenses (rent, books, and food) were relatively small.

I graduated from college in 2005 and moved to New York City—not only the land of opportunity, but also one of the most expensive and distracting cities in the world. I ended up with nearly $20,000 in credit card debt by the time I was in my mid-20s.

And like so many others I've since spoken with, I chose to deal with this debt by ignoring it. I was that adorable ostrich, head in the sand, ass stuck up in the air. Somehow I thought that if I "acted as if," meaning if I maintained the lifestyle I desired as an affirmation of my abundance, that the debt would spontaneously dematerialize. My mom, my aunt, my uncle, and I had founded Team Northrup in 2002, a group of USANA distributors inspired by my mom's work who had heard about the products and the business through her or one of her team members. I was building my business in New York going to networking groups and telling people I taught women about creating financial freedom. People were impressed that this spunky young thing had a successful business and was teaching others how to do the same.

Unfortunately, I soon felt like a huge fraud. I was living in an apartment owned by my mother and I was still racking up credit card debt. What I was portraying on the outside did not match what was actually going on behind the scenes. Yes, I had a great income that came in whether I worked or not because I had spent my summer vacations and Christmas vacations building my business while I was in college. Yet I lacked the practical financial consciousness that would have allowed me to keep any of it. Year after year I had to scramble to pay my taxes (and even had to ask my dad to spot me a few thousand dollars one year to cover them), and I continued to more or less ignore my credit card debt.

♡

Fast-forward a few years. I'm now living in a beautiful home. I paid off all of that debt. I have a nice nest egg growing in the bank, and I'm paying all my living expenses with ease and plenty of cushioning. I have to say it feels damn good.

That's how my money story ends (for now), but there were more than a few twists and turns along the way before I got here.

In 2007 I achieved a coveted rank in the USANA sales force called Gold Director. When you achieve this status in the company they know that you're taking the business seriously because building your business to this level is not for the faint of heart. To reward my efforts, USANA flew me to the Gold Retreat, which was held at the beautiful Canyons Resort in Park City, Utah. Everything was completely five-star: limo service, gifts in the room, flowers, fruit plates, a VIP tour of the Olympic facilities, and lots of pampering.

Going on this trip was an extremely big deal for me because I'd never been treated so well as a result of something I had achieved. Up until this point in my life any trip that was paid for or fancy accommodation I enjoyed was always because I was traveling with my mom and she was being recognized. I brought my mom along for the trip because you could bring a guest, I've always enjoyed her company, and it felt good to be able to share my abundance with her after having been on the receiving end so many times.

At one of our fancy-pants dinners, my mom and I sat next to the president of USANA. In a very hushed tone he told us that he had never suggested what he was about to suggest to any other people in USANA, but we had such a unique situation that he felt we should take advantage of it. Between my mom's reach as a well-known medical expert and my ability to manage the day-to-day aspects of a network marketing business, he felt we would have the perfect partnership. He wowed us with explanations of how we could make significantly more money and help more people together than we could individually. I was enchanted by being picked out of the already elite crew at the Gold Retreat and recognized for my abilities in this way.

After a bit of deliberation, we were both sold. I agreed to stop building my USANA business, which was making a solid mid-five-figure income residually (not so shabby for someone two years out of college), and started focusing all my efforts on my mom's distributorship.

We leapt right in with great enthusiasm and hope. It all seemed like such a great idea. I had the business know-how and the time to do the practical stuff; my mom had the platform to bring lots of people to our team.

But two and a half years into working together I began to feel uneasy. I was having trouble accessing motivation to do the work required to run and build the business. I also started feeling annoyed while training my team, and the process of sponsoring people in the business—a process I had once loved—suddenly exhausted me.

Toward the end of 2010 I had a dream that was simultaneously chilling and illuminating. In the dream I was alive but I had also died. I found my own dead body and for some reason couldn't let anyone know I was dead. I ordered a kit that I found online designed to conceal dead bodies. It was just a plastic bag that sealed to contain the smell (I know, so gross!). I put my body in it and then I somehow fit the whole thing into a FedEx box. I was on my way to an event where I had a Team

Northrup table in the vendor area (something I had done many times in my waking life) and for some reason I had to bring the box containing my body with me. When I got to the event, I created a beautiful display of our product line with my dead-body box as a centerpiece. To ensure that no one knew about my dead body inside that box, I covered the entire table with flowers and sparkles. I also distinctly remember that in this dream I smiled really big throughout the entire event to make sure everything looked okay.

During this time, as you may remember, in my waking life I felt like a fraud because I was traipsing about Manhattan teaching women about financial freedom while I still had (and wasn't doing anything about) some significant consumer debt. There was also the not insignificant detail of living in an apartment that my mother owned and that she paid the mortgage on. Living in the apartment rent-free was part of my compensation for helping build the business, but given that we'd never written out a compensation package or come to a clear agreement, it didn't really feel like I had earned it. It simply felt like I was living in my mom's apartment. The whole time I felt as though I was swimming in a financial quagmire and making a career out of avoidance.

I continued to build my business with my mom, working with women one-on-one to help them create optimal health and financial freedom, mentoring and growing our team, and implementing some new marketing and training strategies that were paying off. But I still had a gnawing feeling that something wasn't right.

The conversations around my business with my mom began to feel more and more strained. Neither of us felt good about where our business or personal relationship was headed. It felt terrible to realize that not only were my mom and I not on the same page, we weren't even in the same book. And it felt particularly terrible to know that I had helped create this situation.

It became painfully obvious that something had to change in my business partnership with my mother, so we decided to finally get some sort of agreement on paper. I presented her with a new proposal for a written agreement of how we could each be compensated for our contribution to the business. The act of quantifying our business and my contribution was incredibly healing and strengthening for me. Once I got clear on how much the business had grown since we began our partnership, I began to see my own value more clearly. I saw that I had brought something to the table and that I wasn't simply riding my mom's coattails. It felt great to see this on a spreadsheet and to also begin to feel it in my cells.

In the midst of this realization, I was beginning to feel called to make some other changes in my living situation. First I decided that I should leave New York and move someplace where I could drastically reduce my living expenses so I could get out of debt and live with more financial integrity. I decided to move to Maine and live with my mom for a few months. I had visions of meeting a lobsterman, getting married, having a few kids, baking pies, and living happily ever after. But just as soon as those visions of domestic bliss in my home state entered my mind's eye, I started to feel contracted and depressed.

One night I was sitting at a restaurant with a very close friend and I got an idea. I would move out of the apartment that I co-owned with my mom but that she paid for, we would sell it, I would get rid of most of my belongings, and I would travel the country on a road trip of indefinite duration. I would call it The Freedom Tour, and I would teach workshops called "Women and Wealth" en route, passing on the keys to financial freedom I had learned along the way to other women. The idea came in a single download, and I felt elated and expansive as I told my friend about it. Her eyes grew wider as I talked. My eyes grew wider. Even our incredibly irritating waitress couldn't break the mood of enthusiasm and possibility.

I knew this was the change I needed. I had a really good life, but it was time for great. I knew that going on The Freedom Tour would drastically decrease my living expenses so I could pay off my debt and begin to live more spaciously around my money. And I already had a successful virtual business with small teams around the country who could host me and put workshops together for me in their hometowns. I didn't know how long I'd go for or where I would land. I was letting go of what I knew, and it felt really, really good.

When we have a shift like this, it's as though a flash flood has washed the path behind us away. If we turn to go back the way we've come, there are no tracks, no clear way to go, and no trace of the old way. So our only choice becomes the choice of moving forward. And move forward, I did! Two weeks before I was to leave and drive from Ellicottville, New York, to San Diego, California, in the middle of February, it occurred to me that I should probably invite someone to drive with me. I was letting go of my life as I knew it, and I was in the middle of a relatively tumultuous time in my relationship with my mother. I would probably need some help, some companionship, and a shoulder to cry on when I woke up somewhere in Oklahoma thinking, *What the hell have I done?!*

So out of nowhere I was inspired to invite this guy Mike who I'd only hung out with a handful of times. We'd met in Chicago the previous June, had e-mailed off and on since then, and had spent time together in Phoenix, where he lived, over Christmas while I was visiting relatives there. It was now January. At the moment of inspiration, a yellow Post-it note quite literally appeared on my mental bulletin board. It said, "Invite Mike Watts to drive across the country with you." And I thought to myself, *What?!?! Who put that there? That's crazy. I barely know the guy.*

But I had to get from Ellicottville to San Diego, and it was the middle of winter, and I was feeling a little shaky in the midst of changing everything in my life. And I had seen Mike Watts's capable arms. They were strong and safe looking—the kind of arms you'd want around if you had a meltdown somewhere in Nebraska. The kind of arms you'd want around if you got stuck in a snowbank in Indiana. And the beautiful thing about changing everything in your life all at once is that it leaves you really open to possibility, so I decided to heed the Post-it. Besides, I'd decided I definitely wasn't going to meet my future husband while crisscrossing the country so I may as well completely follow my desires. With no particular agenda or outcome in mind, I invited Mike to drive with me. He said yes, and within a few days he'd booked a plane ticket from Phoenix to Buffalo to drive a girl he barely knew across the country. There was a blizzard the day he flew in to meet me.

He brought me chocolates. That night he kissed me for the first time, in the living room of the farmhouse where my mom grew up.

On day five of The Freedom Tour, after a conversation negotiating a new business arrangement with my mom, I finally got the clarity I had been listening for. I hung up the phone feeling confused, frustrated, and angry. I walked into my, at the time, very new boyfriend Mike's room with tears streaming down my face, hiccuping my post-sob breaths. After sharing how I felt, Mike looked at me earnestly and asked if he could give me his opinion. I said of course. "Kate, you can do this on your own. You're enough," he said. It was the first time after partnering with my mother that I'd considered going back out on my own. This small taste of freedom, even if only in theory, was delicious.

When I got clear that I no longer wanted to be in business with my mom, I told her with absolute resolve. The conversation lasted less than ten minutes, and it was surprisingly and delightfully easy. She was totally supportive and wished me the best. We untangled ourselves financially over the next six months.

As of September 2011 I am not only completely financially independent and consumer debt–free, I am also completely financially free. My current residual income covers my living expenses so I can choose to work only if I want to for creative fulfillment or to increase my standard of living—we'll cover the full definition of financial freedom in Chapter 8. And, more important, my relationship with my mom is the best it's ever been. We cheer each other on, we hang out with each other just for fun, and we weigh in on each other's business strategies from a place of total love and enthusiasm for the work we're each creating in the world.

As for my Post-it-note guy, I was supposed to drop Mike off five days into the trip at his home in Phoenix. But, to make a long story short, he never got out of the car and we spent the next ten months traveling the country together and fell in love, covering 34,000 miles and 41 states along the way on The Freedom Tour. Now we live together in Maine.

AND NOW . . . YOUR MONEY *LOVE* STORY

Once you've written your story and felt the feelings associated with it, the second stage of the personal money story process is to get into agreement with both your past and your present. One of my all-time favorite teachers, Nicole Daedone, founder of OneTaste and author of *Slow Sex*, once told me that our power in any moment lies in our ability to get into agreement with what's happening—to fall in love with your story. The more we push up against something, the more we find it wrong, and the more we wish it were different, the more powerless we are to create the reality that we desire.

Conversely, the more we embrace the here and now and find ways to appreciate it, and perhaps even be grateful for it, the more power we have to move forward. When we own our money story, and even tell it in such a way that we are the heroine, as opposed to the victim, we lay down the first brushstrokes for our new vision of financial freedom and peace.

Did I just hear you call me a Pollyanna? It's true, there are few places in our culture where we're taught to own the hard parts of our story and choose to see the ways in which they actually worked out perfectly in the larger perspective of our life trajectory. But remember, there's a difference between owning and embracing your story and glossing over grief and hardship. So I'm not suggesting glossing over the hard stuff in order to move right on to feeling good, because the "feeling good" you get to won't last. You need to find those moments in your past that could be looked at as not so good and address them. Find the silver lining. Really look to see what they did *for* you rather than *to* you. And once you start seeing these "bad" things in a new way, you can retell your story with you as the heroine.

So commit now to setting free your woe-is-me. It's time to own your history. It's time to unravel the beauty of your journey up until this point and discover the ways in which it has been a treasure map leading you exactly where you are today. It's time to embrace your story because no amount of wishing it were different will make it so. Instead, tell your story anew. Tell it with magic and awe and a sense of wonder. Tell it proudly because it is the story that has made you who you are. You only get one story this time around, so why not own it?

Now that you know my story, I'd love to show you how I've owned it. How am I the heroine of my story? Well, you saw my twists and turns, my ups and downs, but in the end I have come to realize that by choosing to truly see my value and, as a result, put more value, more of my true voice, out into the world, a lot of great stuff has happened. I paid off all my debt within the course of a few weeks because my income increased so much. I fell in love with an amazing man who totally supports me in work, love, and life and who I support right back.

I started getting paid to speak. I got a book deal (and you're holding the result of it in your hands). I'm doing work that I love, that adds value to my own life, and that improves the lives of others.

If I hadn't gone through that spot I was in even two years ago, I could never have completely embraced, appreciated, or even fully understood being in the spot I am in now. Feeling like a fraud and being in total financial oblivion while amassing interest on my credit cards felt really shitty. The financial consciousness I have now, and the life I'm enjoying as a result, feels amazing. I want this feeling for everyone on the planet. Having gone through my own financial bumps gives me not only the credibility, but also the empathy and perspective to hopefully help thousands of others move through their own versions of money madness with grace and ease.

It turns out that my money story is, in fact, a love story on many levels: it's the story of my love affair with money, the story of an evolution in my loving relationship with my mother, the story of falling in love with my beloved, and the story of helping others create their own money love story.

All of these stories came with their own life lessons, lessons that you sometimes have to search for by looking below the surface of your experiences. For example, let's look at my relationship with my dear dad and how it has shaped my life. My dad was, like my mom, generous with me and my sister over the years, and both of my parents particularly valued education and travel and spared no expense when it came to providing us with academic, artistic, and cultural education throughout our childhoods and teen years. However, my dad has a very different financial constitution than my mother and is generally more conservative with his money. And the truth is, some of his financial choices over the course of my growing years registered emotionally for me as rejection or feeling undervalued, which, in and of itself, is a lesson that I truly appreciate.

One of the greatest lessons I learned came by way of feeling inadequate and not valued. I know what you're thinking—*How could this be positive?* But just stick with me. Unfortunately, as a kid, external circumstances have a tendency to leave indelible marks. This is probably due to a wide variety of factors, including:

1. When you're a kid you're more sensitive and impressionable.

2. As a kid you're completely dependent on your parents or other guardians to get your needs met, so your relationships with them are high-stakes because, on some level, everything that happens with them can potentially affect your survival.

3. You're newer to life as a kid and therefore every experience is fresher and, thus, more viscerally impactful.

4. You don't have the emotional maturity to understand events the same way you do when you become an adult, so you often internalize them in ways that you might not when you're more mature.

All that to say, when I was a kid and teenager and my dad chose not to spend money on me in particular circumstances, I didn't yet have the maturity to talk to him or fully express my feelings about it. Instead, I made a decision early on that would have a ripple effect in my life. I decided that somehow because my dad didn't want to pay for whatever it was, that I was somehow not valuable.

My equating money with love and deciding that I was unlovable because of my interactions with my dad around money basically terrified me away from having meaningful, romantic interactions with men for six and a half years. Of course we both know this is no longer a problem in my life.

Cue the heroine version of the story! What was so perfect about my lack of dating in high school and college was that I saved myself a lot of emotional drama that many young women go through as they navigate the dating world in their late teens and early 20s. Instead, I used my extra emotional energy and spare time to form incredible, long-lasting relationships with girlfriends and to start my own business, which I still reap rewards from more than ten years later.

Have I spent some time and quite a few boxes of Kleenex mourning the loss of my teenage self-worth and the young, fancy-free dating life that I missed out on? You betcha. I've raged. I've journaled. I've danced it out. I've had some amazingly healing heart-to-heart and come-to-Jesus talks with both of my parents and my sister. And I find opportunities to peel back the layers and continue the healing process regularly. But being honest about my feelings doesn't cancel out me being the heroine of this story. After all, what's a good story without some conflict and tears on the other side of the laughter along the way?

All these years later I see that my dad had his own journey around money that had nothing to do with me.

He had a difficult upbringing with some complex dynamics around money and addiction. As a kid I believed that his behavior was connected with how much love I was worth. But that simply isn't true. His choices had, in fact, nothing to do with how he really felt about me or how much he loved me.

And now I choose to see my dad as always having done the best he could with the information, tools, and skills he had available to him. I choose to see him as a loving, generous man who would do anything for me— because that's the truth. And you know what? I'm closer to my dad now than I've been since my age was in the single digits. Our relationship has completely flourished. And guess what else? So have my relationships with other men *and* with my money.

Another way in which I see the perfection in my money love story exactly as it is, is the fact that I owe a great deal of my business and financial success to programming myself for financial freedom at a young age. I am so grateful for this early education. And if it hadn't been for my parents getting divorced and for my mom getting terrified, it's pretty unlikely that I would have turned in my young-adult novels for business and money books.

My rollercoaster ride of being in business partnership with my mother is also hilarious in retrospect. I'm eternally grateful that I didn't know any better than to just dive right in because I was young and innocent and didn't know a thing about anything. This was made manifest in a variety of significant ways, the most important being that we never had a written agreement. Right from the get-go we talked about how I would be compensated and the division of labor, but we never wrote it down and really fleshed it out. This was a huge learning experience for me. I will never, ever again go into a business partnership without putting things in writing, especially with friends or family. But I wouldn't be so firm in my resolve on this point had I not experienced the challenge of what happens when you do it the other way. And the growth that occurred for me personally, and in my relationship with my mom over the course of our business partnership and then separation, is a priceless gift that couldn't have happened any other way. Youthful enthusiasm is such a blessing. It can guide you down the path that your soul requires to grow.

There are so many gems of lessons to pull out from this segment of the story. Not only did I learn to make written agreements, but I also learned that I'm responsible for how much value I put out into the world, and no one else is capable of making me feel smaller than I am unless I let them. I remembered that I'm enough—always have been, always will be. I learned that the things we hold on to in order to keep us safe are often the things that are preventing us from claiming our freedom.

Part of claiming our freedom in any area of our lives is looking at our stories through a lens of seeing the positive lessons, taking responsibility for our part, and finding ways to grow as a result of our experiences. And that's just what I've done.

There are so many reasons I could tell you that could explain why I experienced financial downfalls. I could say it was because I had never been taught financial responsibility by my parents. I could cite that my dad always wanted to teach my sister and me "the value of a dollar" but we would simply go behind his back and ask my mom for money, which she handed out freely. I could say it was because they never shared their financial-planning practices with us, or that I was working out some sort of pain as a result of my parents' divorce and watching the financial upheaval of that.

But the thing is that none of those versions of the story feel particularly freeing. If I were to let my mom or my dad (or society, for that matter) be to blame for getting myself $20,000 in debt, I might as well lock myself into a cell and throw the key out of reach. I was completely responsible for my lackadaisical approach to my finances that left me scrambling, in the red, and ashamed of myself. I chose to not pay attention to my money for a variety of reasons and none of them were anyone else's fault. And it was the perfect twist on my path because there are simply things you can only learn the hard way in order to effectively teach them.

I'm not saying that in order to teach something you have to have been through it (or screwed it up, as the case may be). But let me ask you this: Don't you take me more seriously as a money wisdom teacher knowing that in the span of five years I got myself into and out of nearly $20,000 of debt while building a successful network marketing business? I certainly hope so because writing that sure reminds me that I've got something valuable to teach. This is my heroine version of my story. *I* made mistakes, and *I* overcame them. I am strong and capable. I am living a life much more in line with who I am deep down. My experiences have given me the chance to tune in to my soul's path.

Can you see how valuable a 60,000-foot view of life is from time to time? I once heard Louise Hay say how grateful she is for her ex-husband because even though her heart was broken over their divorce, he made her the Louise Hay she is today. I feel the same way. If my parents hadn't gotten divorced and I hadn't gone through those tough years of watching both my mom and dad be sad, confused, angry, and figuring things out, I never would have learned what I learned to become a successful businesswoman. And I never would have taken the conscious journey to owning my worth and, as a result, adding more value to the planet. I'm so grateful to both of them for everything they've taught me, consciously and unconsciously. It's all worked out exactly as it was supposed to.

I took a few steps that some would see as missteps. If you haven't figured it out yet, I, of course, see all of the moments, all of the choices, all of the happenings as the absolute perfect things to bring me to the very moment I'm in, writing this to you. I don't believe in regret.

WHAT'S YOUR MONEY LOVE STORY?

Now it's your turn! You may be relatively new on the paying-attention-to-your-money path. This may be the first book you've ever read about money. It may be a topic you've avoided most of your life. If so, that's okay. You're doing great! Or perhaps you love this topic and this is one of many resources you've checked out. Either way, now is a great time to take a look at your own money story. This exercise will help walk you through telling your story and then owning it, just like I did above.

Part 1: Tell Your Story

Get out your Money Love Journal and write your own money love story. Where did it all begin? What were the high points? Low points? What were the gems? Tell your money story in a way you've never told it before.

Part 2: Moments to Reframe

Tell the truth, but don't forget your rose-colored glasses. Every moment has been a lesson that has brought you to precisely where you are today. Where in your life have you let a challenging circumstance or event define your reality? Where have you not taken responsibility for the way you're choosing to see something? Pick one or two such areas of your money story, and look for ways in which things really have ended up perfectly as a result of these circumstances that may not have felt so great at the time. Did you learn something you couldn't have learned in the same way without getting into debt? Did you begin to claim your financial power or your worth in a new way after realizing how painful it had become to give it away? I'm not asking you to completely switch your perspective on whatever unpleasant circumstances might be hanging out in your past. But I am asking you to do a quarter turn. Is there one thing from your money story you can choose to find right in this moment? Maybe even two?

Part 3: Heroine's Journey Version of the Story

Today is the day to own your story and get into agreement with how things are. And that starts by acknowledging the beauty and perfection of the path you've walked to get here. Now I invite you to expand upon the approach we took in Part 2. Now that you've shifted your perspective on a particular element or two of your money story, take an overview of your story as a whole and look for more layers of perfection and beauty and rightness in what *is* (and/or *was*). You can freewrite on this, meditate on it and ask whatever you consider to be your Higher Power for guidance, or discuss it with a trusted friend who has an evolved perspective. Or you can do all three. Once you start to nudge your perspective on things in a new direction, you may be surprised by how your life can begin to unfold itself before you like a rich, gorgeous tapestry, the pain and the joy, the grace and the growth all woven together perfectly and inextricably. Just like it did with mine, your perspective shifting may come to include other aspects of your life beyond your relationship with money. Everything in life is, after all, interconnected. Whatever you do, do yourself the honor of telling your story with you as the heroine. You are absolutely worth that distinction.

Chapter 2

IT'S NOT ABOUT THE MONEY

Since the whole money system is made up, why not be a participant instead of a bystander? Or instead of a victim? Everywhere you go you can hear people complaining about the state of the economy and being victims of their circumstances:

"Oh, unemployment is at ten percent, the highest since nineteen-twenty-nine, so there's no way I can increase my income, let alone get a job."

"People with my education just don't make more than thirty thousand dollars a year. They never have and they never will."

"There's no way I'm starting a business. It's risky. Do you know how bad the economy is?"

I'm sure you have your own go-to statement for why you can't, won't, or don't have what you want.

Becoming aware of the cockamamie things we tell ourselves that keep us stuck is actually incredibly helpful and transformative. Awareness is the first step to change.

So air it out. And notice when your stinkin' thinkin' or stinkin' talkin' is coming out.

THE VOICES IN YOUR HEAD

Let's be honest. The fact that you picked up this book means you're someone who's at least somewhat (and probably more than somewhat) aware of her thoughts, beliefs, and emotions. You may have read the above examples of financial whimpering and thought to yourself, *Oh, I don't think like that. I know that I consciously create my own reality. I'm not a victim. I'm an exception to the norm.*

Have you ever said or thought, "I can't afford that?" If so, you may want to take a closer look at just how much you believe you create your own reality. Even those of us who've spent hours working with life coaches, attended hundreds of personal growth seminars, read everything published by Hay House, and logged a lot of time with our butts on a meditation cushion can't claim perfection when it comes to those little voices in our head.

The second step to changing your reality around money is simply becoming aware of your thoughts about it. Why? Because our thoughts create our beliefs, which create our actions, which in turn create our reality. This is just the way it is. And where do those thoughts come from? My lord, they come from everywhere! The media, our parents, the snot-nosed kid in second grade who called us fat, our bosses, and our sometimes-not-so-friendly minds. If we don't pay attention to the thoughts that are creating our beliefs, our actions, and ultimately, our realities, we're not actually in charge of our lives. Instead we're letting some random reporter from the eleven o'clock news, or possibly even worse, our mothers or fathers, run our lives.

As I traveled the country during The Freedom Tour doing Women and Wealth workshops with over 800 participants, I heard some pretty amazing things when it got to the moment in the evening when we talked about what we heard about money while growing up. One of my all-time favorites was: "It's just as easy to fall in love with a rich man as a poor man." Other common ones were, "Money doesn't grow on trees," and of course, the old favorite, "We can't afford that."

What I love about this step is that it's incredibly simple. Become aware. Okay, I can do that. You don't have to give your retirement plan an overhaul and draw up a genius spending plan (though you may choose to do that as part of your financial freedom plan later on). But for today, for right now, let's start with simply becoming aware of the mishegas about money that is running our financial lives, whether we like it or not.

This is the point in our time together when I'm going to hold your hand as you unravel some stuff. Geneen Roth, best-selling author of the book and course, *Women, Food and God*, among others, wrote: "The only people who don't have insane relationships with money are those who were willing to examine their insane relationships with money." Genius and oh so true.

So let's put on our detective caps à la Sherlock Holmes (I find everything is easier if I wear the right outfit, especially when it comes to money) and let the awareness roll!

HEARING THE VOICES

Grab your Money Love Journal because we're about to reach the next layer of awareness. Start to listen to, identify, and decode the voices in your head in regard to money. Begin to listen to your repetitive thoughts about money—you'll find that many of them are not actually being said in your voice. Now write down what you heard people (generally adults) saying about money when you were growing up. Begin to notice how many times throughout the day you say these exact same things.

How do you like peeling back the layers on this particularly juicy onion? Are you feeling excited or getting curious? Maybe yes. Maybe no. If you're finding yourself getting stressed-out, worried, annoyed with me, sleepy, or foggy, just remember that these are all signs of resistance. And guess what? If you're having any of the signs of resistance come up, it's actually good news. My dear friend and mentor Barbara Stanny, author of the book and course, *Overcoming Underearning*, says that our degree of resistance around money is proportional to the degree of power available to us on the other side of that resistance.

So that means the more frustrated, irritated, or spaced-out around your money you are, the more power is available to you financially when you're willing to work through that resistance. Remember, I spent a good four years traipsing around New York City teaching women about financial freedom while ignoring my mounting credit-card debt. I so know resistance. And I'm reporting back from the other side of my resistance to let you know that Stanny is right: there's a lot of power over here! So, remain present by getting into your body. Feel your butt in your chair, get up and do a hip circle or two, take a dance break, and then come on back because we've got some important work to do.

YOUR FIRST MONEY MEMORY

In this next step, we're going to delve even deeper into how our childhoods have come to bear in our present financial lives. When I was traveling the country, I heard astounding stories in my workshops of women realizing that their current financial circumstances were a very clear mirror of their childhood circumstances. It might be 10, 20, or even 40 years since you were a kid, but you can still be re-creating the experiences you had as a child.

Rosie was a beautiful woman in her 40s who attended one of my Women and Wealth workshops and had a huge "aha" moment. She had always dated men who were broke and ungenerous. They were wonderful men otherwise, but there was always a hang-up around money. She was currently married to a great guy, but no matter what he did he could never seem to get it together financially. She felt totally burdened by this and was frustrated. She didn't want to leave the marriage just because of money, yet she longed to be taken care of financially. For her, men and money had never mixed well and this was the biggest sticking point in her marriage and her number one money frustration.

As we worked together Rosie began connecting the dots between her childhood experiences and her present-day. She remembered a time when she was seven years old and had witnessed a heated discussion between her parents. Her father had raised his voice at her mother, reprimanding her for buying clothes that day, which he saw as frivolous. "I don't work my ass off all day to pay for you to waltz around, lunch with your friends, and spend my money!" he chastised her. Rosie remembered her mother looking at him in fear, apologizing very quietly, and timidly tiptoeing out of the room to escape his anger.

Rosie recalled making a vow to herself to never be in a position where she was dependent upon a man for money. She didn't want to turn into her mother. But she realized that she had swung the pendulum too far the other direction. Instead of being beholden to a man, she had created relationship after relationship where she was with men who weren't in a position to support her. So, in essence, she had on some level re-created the emotional experience of not being cared for that she saw her mother go through. And now that she was aware of the pattern she could look at ways to consciously transform her relationship with her husband and money instead of using it as an unconscious playground for her childhood wounds and contracts.

CONNECTING THE DOTS

Part 1: Your Money Memory

Close your eyes. Take three deep breaths in and out through your nose. Ask yourself what your first, or most powerful, memory from your childhood is that has to do with money. Who was there? What words did you hear? What were the circumstances? How did you feel? Take another slow, deep breath through your nose and then slowly open your eyes. Write down what you recalled in your Money Love Journal.

Part 2: Your Top Money Frustration

Now we're moving into the present day. Becoming aware of your thoughts and actions around money starts with simply being honest with yourself about where you're frustrated. In the last chapter we rewrote our money stories so you're already learning to get into agreement with where you're at. But, even if you're in agreement with it, it still may be frustrating that you owe $15,000 in credit-card debt or that you never seem to have enough money to cover your bills at the end of the month. Now, write down your number one money frustration.

Part 3: Making the Connection

Look at your top money frustration, and then review the story you wrote about your first memory about money. Is there a connection? If so, where do you see the connection? Write it down.

If you didn't see a direct connection between your childhood memory and your current financial reality, don't worry. Sometimes there is no direct connection. It doesn't mean that our exploration together isn't working. Clarity is power and clarity comes first from awareness. So, keep paying attention to your thoughts and asking where those thoughts are coming from.

CHANGING YOUR VIEW

If you want to change your reality, you need to start with your thoughts. Changing your perception of your current financial frustrations is an excellent place to get this going.

My good friend Marie Forleo made a great point about one of the most common phrases I hear at my workshops—and one of the situational misperceptions that you can work on: "I can't afford that." Marie said she noticed when her business first started taking off that she thought she should be living in a multimillion dollar townhouse in the West Village in New York City instead of the apartment she was living in at the time. Though at first she said to herself, "Yeah, but I can't afford a home like that," she soon realized that this wasn't entirely the case. After looking a bit more closely at the situation, Marie realized that the truth was not that she couldn't afford it (though she didn't have several million in the bank at the time, it was true), but that she didn't want to do what it would take to get a multimillion dollar home at that particular point in time.

When I was first beginning my USANA business in college, I enrolled a woman named Leah who had immigrated to the United States from the Caribbean. Leah was a hairdresser who often worked ten or more hours a day, six days a week. She lived in a working-class coastal town and didn't have a lot of extra money to throw around. She always looked incredibly beautiful and chic and she and I both knew she would be a customer magnet, particularly with our skin-care line.

After I presented the business to Leah she told me that she was really excited to work with me but she didn't have the money to get started. She did, however, have a big network of friends, family, and clients whom she wanted to tell about the products immediately. So, she and I worked together to create a beautiful gathering at her salon where everyone got to have a mini facial and get completely pampered by Leah. Every single attendee ordered product and Leah collected $2,000 worth of orders that night, more than enough to get her business started.

Leah had a great view of her financial situation. Instead of complaining about the fact that she didn't have the exact amount of money, she got to work putting what she had of value into action to get what she wanted. She had a salon. She had a supportive network. She had a gift for making people feel beautiful and cared for. So instead of saying, "I can't afford it" when I told her how much it would cost to start her business, she went about making it happen because she valued it enough.

The truth is when you really, really, really want something so badly it makes you sweat a little bit when you think about it, you will do whatever it takes to get it. You will sell your stuff. You will get a part-time job. You'll borrow the money. You'll figure out a way. And when you realize that this is possible, you change your view of your current circumstances. You bring desire coupled with faithful action. And this rich combination makes things happen.

WANTING IT ENOUGH

Think of a time in your life when you wanted something like crazy. Your mouth watered every time you thought about it. It was in your daydreams. It was in your dreams at night. You Googled it a million times a day. You had an intense desire.

Let's say that this thing you wanted like crazy was a plane ticket to fly across the country to see this guy who you were nuts about. Now, technically the money wasn't in your bank account. But your desire to get your cute butt across the country and see that fine man was so strong that you were willing to do whatever it would take to get on that plane. So you spent a Saturday afternoon combing your closet for all the designer-sample-sale finds you didn't wear that often, jogged on down to the consignment store, and walked out with a few crisp hundred-dollar bills with Virgin America's name on them.

> I know you can think of a time when you wanted some-
> thing so much that you found a way to make it happen. So,
> when you find yourself feeling victimy and whiny and hear
> yourself say the words "I can't afford that," remember: It's
> not about the money. If you really wanted it you would fig-
> ure out a way to get it. If it were that VALUABLE to you, you
> would make it happen. So it's not that you can't afford it.
> It's just that you don't value it enough to do what it would
> take to get it. From here on out you can replace the phrase
> "I can't afford that" with "How can I afford that?" or "I'm
> choosing not to buy that," because that's really the truth.

If your frustration with your financial circumstances doesn't lie simply in the thought *I can't afford
that,* it's important that you focus on reframing what's
bothering you. You've already proven to yourself that
much of your circumstance lies in your perception of
your financial life. So let's rework some of the other
views you have about your circumstances using a
much-employed tool of the self-help trade: affirmations, or mantras.

I want to be super clear here. Affirmations are not
magical incantations that make things happen. The way
I like to think of them, instead, is as touchstones. For
example, the other day I was in a tizzy about having
too much to do. I felt like I was running out of time, I
didn't know where to start, I felt deadlines weighing on
me, and I was totally overwhelmed. In that moment I
remembered something my cousin Rachel told me one
day as we were working out. During the toughest parts of
our workout, she had used the mantra "I am pure, calm
grace" to move through the time. When I caught myself
in the downward thought spiral about having too much

to do, I stopped myself and instead repeated the words "I am pure, calm grace" in my head over and over.

Guess what? I felt better. And you know what happens when we move toward a thought that feels better by choosing an affirmation or mantra? We make better choices. We make more empowered choices. The world becomes our oyster rather than our rotten, smelly clam.

I don't believe you can affirm your way out of feeling emotions that don't feel good. Sometimes you just need to feel downright rotten. Sometimes, the only way out is through.

But there's a difference between fully feeling your feelings and getting caught in an unproductive, negative downward thought spiral. I'm sure you've heard the statistic before that on average, 80 percent of our thoughts are negative. And even more alarming, 95 percent of them repeat throughout the day.

So the idea with mantras, or touchstones, is to give us a place to come back to when we notice that our train of thought has veered off track. When we keep our minds coming back to a place that feels good, we feel good. When we feel good, we make better choices. When we make better choices, our life ends up feeling better more often. And this applies to our financial lives 100 percent.

DRAWING UP NEW PLANS

Write your top money frustration again here: _____

_____

_____.

Now it's time for some retooling. Take your top money frustration from above and rewrite it so that it's flipped into a positive mantra. Here's an example:

Money frustration: I never have enough money.

Flipped into an affirmation: I always have more than enough money to do the things I want to do.

Write your flipped frustration as a new money mantra in your Money Love Journal.

If you find yourself not believing the mantra, tweak it a little bit. The reason "I am pure, calm grace" works so well for me is that my unconscious mind can believe it—no matter what is happening in my outside world. So flipping your money frustration into something like "I trust that I will be abundantly provided for all of my days" may feel more true than "I always have more than enough money to do the things I want to do."

Make your money mantra a calming, feel-good thought that is also believable.

While you're in the mind-set of flipping thoughts to more positive versions that will actually serve you on your financial journey, why not do a few more to get some additional practice? Do three or more financial frustrations flipped into money mantras in your Money Love Journal.

So there it is. You've started to change your thoughts about your situation and about what's possible moneywise. Now it's time to start changing your thoughts about something a little more personal—something that will affect you on an even deeper level. It's time to examine your thoughts about *you*. Your beliefs about what you are worth and how money plays into that equation have a huge impact on your money love story.

THE INSIDE JOB

I was cruising at 35,000 feet, somewhere above the Midwest. I was winging my way back from San Diego to New York City, journal open on my tray table, pen in hand, ink gliding across the beautiful, lavender, hand-made-paper page. I was on my second round through Barbara Stanny's Overcoming Underearning workshop, only this time I was doing the phone version instead of the in-person version.

Let me take a step back and let you in on something. I am a personal-growth junkie. I grew up going to the Omega Institute with my mom when she taught workshops there, and ever since I was hooked. I'm a four-time graduate of Mama Gena's School of Womanly Arts; during The Freedom Tour I managed to get in eight weekends focused on personal growth, not to mention the workshops I was teaching. If you're offering something that's going to help me get to know myself better, enhance my relationships, and possibly give me more skills and information to be happier, more in love, more abundant, more present, healthier, or feel better, I'm in!

But, with my zealous nature often comes a lack of follow-through. One of the telltale ways this shows up is that I don't fully (or even partially) do the homework or exercises during classes. This particular winter, though, I had made a commitment to myself to attend every single call that Stanny was leading, as well as complete every single exercise, not just in my head (as I usually did) but on paper.

I was finally starting to get it that if I didn't start paying some serious attention to my money that not only would my credit-card debt not decrease to zero anytime soon, I would probably continue to rack it up. My discomfort around my financial woe was becoming significant enough to finally make me commit to myself and pay attention to my money.

So on that fateful day, zipping through the stratosphere, I had a realization about the way I was dealing with money (or really not dealing with it) that changed me on a cellular level. Here's what I wrote:

I'd better digest . . . I feel like I might levitate off my seat from all the energy and motivation I'm feeling right now. I think I've truly committed to myself around my money in my business in a really, really powerful way. I feel a shift. I feel a true shift and like things are possible now that weren't possible before—like I can really grow and expand in a HUGE way this year. There's no good reason not to. And having the self-love to prioritize myself and my money, and to take care of my money and myself will only be laying the foundation for huge expansion and stretching and growth beyond my wildest dreams. I get it that this is about putting ME FIRST. And part of that is spending less than I make. And that is a way of loving myself in the most exquisite and powerful way possible. Reading *Overcoming Underearning* and *Getting to I Do* simultaneously has been so powerful for getting it about self-love in a new way. Pat Allen talks about loving yourself more than your man and enough to choose what's right for you. And taking care of my money is about becoming my own Prince Charming. It's about having enough self-love to say yes to me first and no to anything that doesn't serve me. I've only heard this a million times but this time I've heard it in a new way.

I get it that prioritizing myself and my well-being is the only way to get what I want—even writing about it makes me feel SO POWERFUL, like no matter what happens I've got me and that's not only enough, it's everything. That unshakable self-love that will get me where I'm going—treasuring myself above all. It will get me to financial freedom by age 30 in a way that overspending, overplanning, overscheduling and not taking time out for my priorities, buying clothes, not being aware of my money, and all the other ways I have dimmed my light in the past . . . not speaking up, playing small, hanging out with non-empowering friends, shrinking around successful people and being intimidated, judging myself for building a business connected to Mom's success, staying in debt, being addicted to looking perfect, overdrawing my checking account . . . never could have. I GET IT!!!

I've told so many people that at the root of all problems is a lack of self-love, but it never occurred to me that my money challenges had anything to do with that and that taking care of myself in this way has nothing to do with deprivation or limitation but EVERYTHING TO DO WITH SELF-LOVE! I am so ready to walk this path with myself by my side (and my huge community of supporters). I am ready to enter the world of high earners and savvy money managers. It's like I just took off a pair of glasses that were the wrong prescription and I'm seeing straight for the first time. DUH! This is important. This is top-of-the-priority-list important. This is my life, my relationship with myself, and my self-love we're talking about. Not only is this PART of my success, this is the foundation without which the other things can never occur.

I am a genius for conjuring this class with Barbara (as a gift no less!) and for being willing to GO HERE! I've been tracking my spending, I JOURNALED (huge for me because I've been so resistant to journaling in the past), I looked at my earnings and expenses from last year, I fired my bookkeeper and decided it's important for me to keep my books myself (at least for a while), and I'm actively working this program. I think this is the first time I've done a personal-growth program/book and actually DONE IT. Like "full-on" done it. Before I've avoided the exercises and homework, thinking doing it in my head is just as good and that I already know this stuff, but boy was I wrong!

Dropping my ego let me expand and grow into a much deeper, higher place of discovery and love and compassion for myself—and POWER! I feel like I could pick up a car right now! I can't wait to get off this plane and get home so I can clean out my closets and get to work. This day is a turning point . . . and forward I glide into my magnificent future. I no longer see living within my means as limiting and deprived; I see it as loving myself. I now love myself by living abundantly and joyfully within my means. How amazing!

As I wrote, I realized that my lack of financial attention was actually about a lack of self-love. These two subjects are so intensely intertwined that I couldn't believe I hadn't realized this before. If you can't see your value, the world doesn't give value back. For me, this manifested through debt. I didn't feel worthy of the extra time and attention necessary to live within my means, so I lived without financial integrity. And to be honest, there was a part of me that felt like crap about this.

My lack of financial awareness was a way of throwing myself under the bus. I kept myself smaller than necessary by not opening my credit-card statements, spending more than I made, overdrawing my checking account, and putting others' needs in front of my own. I was still learning to value my contributions in the world, my insights, my ideas, my creativity, and my basic value as a woman. I was still pretty shaky in this area and my lack of financial well-being was a reflection of my lack of self-value and self-love.

When I first became aware of the way my shaky self-value was manifesting in my life, I was simultaneously shocked and energized by the information. Now that I had realized how I viewed myself, I knew I could change it. By addressing my lack of self-love, I was also addressing my financial problems.

We often think that if we would just create the perfect budget, master spreadsheet-making, get the right job, hire the perfect business coach, read *The Wall Street Journal,* become an investing wiz, and/or learn to balance our checkbook with joy and ease, we would have it all figured out. But that's just not true.

Have you heard the stories of the people who win the lottery and then are completely broke again three years later? Conversely, you know how Donald Trump has been bankrupt something like nine times and yet he always seems to become a billionaire again? Why is that?

It's because it's not about the money. Remember, money doesn't exist. Money is simply a stand-in for what we value, and often it's a stand-in for how much we value ourselves. Someone who is barely getting by and spends his last two dollars on a winning lottery ticket is not hard-wired for abundance, and the sudden influx of money isn't enough to re-do his wiring. Donald Trump, on the other hand, is completely and totally wired for the big bucks.

Do you think it's a coincidence that as soon as I dismantled my business partnership with my mom and started seeing how valuable I was that I started making more money than I had ever made in my life? And that I got a book deal? I don't think so. Money flows to those who value themselves. Plain and simple.

It doesn't matter how perfectly you budget or what color highlighter you use as you pick apart *Money* magazine. If you don't start with the inner stuff, the outer stuff won't matter. You'll end up the person who hits it big only to lose it a year or less later because she hadn't reorganized her own personal value to reflect the huge influx of monetary value.

How annoying is it that everything worth having starts as an inside job? Want a love affair that will rock your world? Start by loving yourself. Want your boss to take you seriously as a contender for that incredible promotion? Start by taking yourself seriously. Want to be acknowledged for the myriad ways in which you add value to the organization you devote your precious time and energy to? Start by giving yourself a big old pat on the back for your contributions.

When it comes to money, it's the same darn thing. It doesn't matter if your desire is to be debt-free and make $50,000 per year or if it's to be a multimillionaire. The path is the same. It starts with you.

The most important asset you have in life is you, so why not bring out the big guns and just start there?

VALUING YOURSELF

Creating more value in your life, financially and otherwise, starts with valuing yourself. We're going to take a moment right now to own how incredible you are. Research from The School of Positive Psychology, which I read about in *The Happiness Advantage* by Shawn Achor, tells us that it takes 21 days of doing something new for it to become a habit that we don't even have to think about doing anymore. Let today be day one of your new habit of valuing yourself.

Grab your Money Love Journal and write down three specific things you value about yourself. Writing down "I'm healthy" as something you value about yourself is great, but it doesn't stir the same emotional response as if you're really specific. For example, I could write that "I have strong, toned legs that get me from place to place" as something I value about myself. Yes, it's related to my health and it's part of that, but it's more specific and immediately makes me feel more valuable than simply writing "my health."

When you're done, get out your calendar. Create a repeating event for every morning just when you wake up or every evening just before you go to bed (this works best if you use something digital like Google Calendar that will text you or pop up on your computer with a reminder). Then when you see that event on your calendar or the reminder pops up, grab your journal and write down three new things you value about yourself. It doesn't have to take long. Just do it. No excuses.

Make sure to be specific. Don't repeat something from the day before. I promise, there's an infinite supply of reasons you're amazing and truly valuable, so finding three new ones each day is not only possible, it will also become fun and easy as you form the habit.

This exercise will take less than five minutes a day but the return on the time spent will pay you very prettily, financially and otherwise. If you do this for 21 days, you'll have formed a solid foundation for valuing yourself. Notice what happens. Notice how you feel. Notice how the people in your life respond. Your time and energy spent valuing yourself will not only positively impact your own financial life, it will actually make everyone else's life around you better, too. Continue this practice daily beyond the 21 days to really see the investment begin to pay off.

As I was addressing my lack of self-love, I started to realize a number of important things, including how closed off I was from receiving value. Being open to receiving value is actually a form of self-love—and one that many of us have problems with. Here's a classic scenario: You go out for coffee with a girlfriend, and she tells you that today it's on her, but you refuse to let her pay. You argue with her. You put your foot down. You won't let her buy that $3.50 latte. You're not allowing yourself to receive the value she's trying to give you.

Or perhaps at work you deflect a compliment from your co-worker: "This dress? Oh, it was on sale. It's no big deal." Maybe you refuse to let someone open the door for you or pull out your chair. You don't say a genuine thank you when someone tells you they appreciate something. You push it away. You make excuses. You diffuse it with self-deprecation.

Once I realized that I was doing this, I also realized it had to stop. My attitude wasn't good for me.

I was devaluing myself, telling myself I wasn't worth these offers. And by doing this, I was blocking the flow of abundance—remember, if you can't see your value, the world doesn't give value back. So I began expanding my capacity to receive. When I got a compliment, I would pause, look the person in the eye, breathe deeply into my belly, and say "Thank you." That's really all you have to do. Once you master this, you can start doing other receiving—accepting a dinner invitation, saying thank you, and enjoying the full gift; answering the question of what you want for your birthday with a thank you and some ideas; taking a friend up on their offer of help that will truly make your life better. By doing this, you're making it easy for the world to bestow the riches of love, acknowledgment, gifts, and even money upon you by fully receiving it—and you're showing yourself love.

LEARNING TO RECEIVE

Take a moment and recall a compliment that someone gave you recently. Perhaps you shrugged it off in the moment or deflected it. Now, remember the compliment and open your arms wide to physically receive it. It doesn't matter if you didn't fully receive it when it was given. Now is your chance. Take a deep breath and really take in what that other person took the time to point out that they value about you. Feel how good that feels, even if it's a little uncomfortable. The next time someone pays you a compliment (and I chose the word *pays* on purpose), pause, take a deep breath, and give them a sincere thank you. Fully receive their compliment so you can allow yourself and them to be in the flow of abundance.

As I was working on my perception of myself with my affirmations, my calendar pop-ups, and my receiving practices, my perceptions about the relationship between money and self-love began to shift—specifically I came to realize that paying attention to my money was actually a profound act of self-love. Attention is love. Love is attention. And when this bolt of lightning hit me, I found that I had been living with an erroneous belief that spending within my means and paying attention to my money would exhibit a lack mentality—a mentality where you believe that there's not enough to go around. I thought that if I paid attention to my expenses it meant I was worried about not having enough, so I just ignored them and went into overdraft and debt instead. I thought that living within my means meant I suddenly had to start wearing burlap jumper dresses that made me look like a refrigerator. It felt so unsexy to me.

But this wasn't true, and so I started to make some pretty dramatic changes in my life that allowed me to turn up the volume on my voice and speak up more. When I left New York City on The Freedom Tour and unraveled my business with my mom, I was suddenly in a position to show myself what I was made of. And this resulted in more powerfully honing my message in workshops, more boldly telling people the truth (with love), doing more writing, and basically putting more of my real self and what I really thought and felt into the world. I found out that I didn't need to be attached to anyone else to make my opinions credible or valuable. I found out that my showing up as myself, with my perspectives, thoughts, opinions, and presence was not only enough, it was valuable. And the world began to reflect that back to me with more opportunities (speaking gigs, book deals, fun things to participate in) and more money. Here's the equation:

*self-value + paying attention to your money
+ giving more value = receiving more value.*

Very cool.

GIVING VALUE AND SELF-LOVE

I'll be first to admit that I love saying yes to people and being part of something bigger than myself. When someone asks me to do something, my knee-jerk answer is always yes. And this tendency has gotten me into a lot of trouble over the years because I've ended up having a schedule filled with things that have to do with other people instead of a schedule at least partially filled with things that have to do with caring for myself and making sure I get what I need. And this is not a good idea when it comes to giving and receiving value. When you're tired and have put no focus on yourself, the value you give isn't that valuable. And that means that value doesn't come back to you. So giving value, and in turn receiving value, is a great deal about self-love. This is another mind-set that many people need to work to change. Remember what I said about this being an inside job?

My friend Gene is a great example of someone who is on a learning curve around over-giving versus giving value. She is on multiple nonprofit boards, runs two companies, is an advisor to several more start-ups, consults with an NGO in a developing country in Asia, and has one of the most thriving social lives I've ever witnessed. And, she's a single mom. Every time I visit her home it's chaos. There are toys blocking the front door. Clothes are flung everywhere. Several times when I've watched her kids for her and I've given them baths, I've realized the only clean towels in the house were a few washcloths.

Luckily Gene is incredibly energetic, but I can see her behavior of saying yes to everyone, which by default means saying no to some of her own basic needs (and those of her family), beginning to wear thin on her health and spiritual well-being. As she's begun to include one long weekend a month that's completely unplugged to spend with her kids or on her own, without any business going on, I can see not only how she's becoming a softer, more grounded person, but how she's actually beginning to make smarter business decisions that make more money. Coincidence? I think not.

It's no secret that most people, especially women, put themselves last on their lists. Lack of self-care is practically an epidemic. Women who don't put themselves at the top of their priority list are on the one hand applauded by society for being so selfless, nurturing, and giving, and then on the other hand are completely having their energy drained until they're running on fumes in their daily life.

It's probably not news to you that self-care is important, but I bet you've pooh-poohed the advice to spend more time and energy on caring for yourself because you've immediately assumed that doing so would be too expensive. You think of spending the day at the spa, expensive lunches with girlfriends, and yoga retreats in Bali. Yeah, those things are all great for a vision board, but who has the time or money for them? So you go back to your old ways, saying yes to volunteering to chaperone at the upcoming field trip and yes to that extra project at work, even though it means more hours for no more pay. When your boyfriend asks you if you can read through a report he needs to hand in the next day, you say yes, even though your eyes are burning from spending the day in front of the computer and you're desperate to sleep. You say yes to your girlfriend who asks you to help plan her wedding and you say yes to your co-worker who asks if you can help organize the stockroom over the weekend. And you get more tired, more burned out, and more lost to yourself.

The distinction between over-giving and giving more value is a bit subtle, but it's really important, so let's take a moment to look at it together now. I like to think of it like two different kinds of water sources. Giving value to the world feels like a fountain where the water spurts out and then falls back into a holding vessel and then gets recycled back into the system to come out again in the fountain. It's a perpetual source of water, and it's a great metaphor for our own energy and creativity. Giving value to the world feels like this—you have plenty more to give and it's sustainable and feels nourishing to you at the same time as you're nourishing others. Then there are fountains like a sprinkler where the water is just shooting into the grass and it's not sustainable. The source is never replenished. This is what over-giving feels like. Eventually your energetic and creative reserves get depleted and it's exhausting. It takes practice to know the difference between these two types of giving. Giving in a way that nourishes you adds value and is of service to others. Giving your value in a way that saps your energy or is depreciated or isn't reciprocated or fully valued is not truly in service to the greater good. Basically, one type of giving feels good and one doesn't—it's that simple. You may already know the difference within yourself but, if not, you can start being on the lookout for this and you'll start to feel it in different situations in your life.

In my life, when I was working with my mom on Team Northrup, I began to resent putting time and energy giving value in that arena because the partnership wasn't working anymore. In contrast, when I began to write weekly blog posts, do public speaking, and write this book, I was working harder in many ways, giving a lot more value and helping a lot more people, but instead of feeling exhausted and stressed-out, I felt nourished by it.

So what does self-care have to do with money? Everything. Remember, you're trying to change your thoughts about you—to open your eyes to your worth. Dedicating time to care for yourself shows you that you are worth caring for. You are worth working for. You are worth loving, and when you realize this, you are able to give more value, which in turn brings more value into your life.

So, I'm here to tell you that self-care does not have to be expensive, and it doesn't even have to take a lot of time. I'm not saying that these things are bad; they just aren't necessary. No time and no money are the two biggest reasons you'll give me as to why you can't do it. And I'm here to gently and lovingly drive it into that beautiful head of yours that you can. Because your life depends on it.

So let's really look at self-care and self-love. For some, it might conjure up images of lolling about in bed all day eating bonbons, or even some sort of sex workshop for women in the 1970s about learning to have orgasms on their own (Betty Dodson anyone?). The idea of self-love might make you squeamish or uncomfortable. You might think that spending time, energy, and god forbid money (though I just told you, this is not required) is selfish.

Let me break it down for you. Most women on this planet could stand to be a little more selfish if you ask me. But, given that the word *selfish* has such a negative connotation in our culture, let me tell you why caring for yourself and self-love are perhaps the least selfish things you could do. Here are five really good reasons to care for yourself as a way of practicing self-love:

1. You cannot give of an empty cup. If you're trying to pour someone a beverage out of a container that has nothing in it, how is that person going to quench their thirst? They're not. You're SOL (shit out of luck) because you've got nothin'. The person you're trying to give to is SOL because they've got nothin'. When you've got nothing left, you have nothing to give. This is not rocket science. It's simple physics. A three-year-old could understand this concept. And yet women (and men) around the planet are trying to squeak out every last bit of juice they have to give to someone else, leaving themselves with nothing.

2. Not caring for yourself makes you cranky. When you're cranky you're no good to anyone else. Have you ever heard the saying "If Mama ain't happy, ain't nobody happy"?

Of course you have. It's ubiquitous because it's true. Your emotional tenor affects the people around you. If you've not taken any energy to make sure you're taken care of *before* you make sure everyone else has been taken care of, you're no good to anyone *and* you'll make them cranky, too.

3. Martyrdom is so 1250. Yes, there have been times in history when martyrs became saints and were applauded for their sacrifices. But it was usually after their death and usually after tremendous suffering. Again, what good are you to anyone if you're dead, or at the very least, incapacitated? No good.

4. Suffering does not buy you anything. Yes, we've heard it before. "No pain, no gain." "What doesn't kill you makes you stronger," so we could drill it into our psyches even deeper. Do I believe that challenges in life are inevitable? Yes. But is suffering a requirement? Nope. Somewhere along the way we've gotten the message that the more we struggle and the more we suffer, the more valuable we will become and the more successful we'll eventually be. And so we overwork ourselves, overschedule ourselves, and become "busier than thou" because we think there's some sort of prize on the other side of the pain we cause ourselves. And you know what? There's no prize. All you get from suffering is more suffering.

No one is waiting in heaven to give you a medal for being the most hardworking, the most over-giving, and the most emotionally and spiritually starved woman to walk the earth. Ain't gonna happen, honey. As Kris Carr so brilliantly wrote in *Crazy Sexy Diet*, "Stress is not . . . a badge of courage."

5. Exhaustion, stress, and burnout do not result in good work. The entire premise of this book is that if we create financial freedom for ourselves, the extra mental, emotional, and spiritual space we free up will allow us to operate as our best selves in this lifetime. Your best self cannot shine through if you're constantly burdened by putting others before yourself. Your best self likes naps and massages and time to play. Your best self does her best work when she's nourished, well hydrated, has lots of pleasure in her life, and has slept at least eight hours. Your magnum opus will be far more likely to emerge after a hot roll in the hay (with yourself or a partner) than after pulling an all-nighter to get a project done for your boss.

Have I made myself clear? Self-care is not about pretty throw pillows and spa appointments (though these are also lovely when you can purchase them in a financially sound way). Self-care is about loving yourself. If you can't learn to put energy toward your own care and feeding, who else will? If you can't value yourself enough to put yourself first from time to time, how the heck do you expect to be valued in the world?

Money is about what we value. We pay for what we value. We pay attention to what we value. This is an issue of valuing yourself.

I don't think there's a moment where we arrive and we've learned to love or value ourselves enough. And the path of self-value, paying attention to our money, giving value, and receiving value isn't linear. It's a give-and-take. Sometimes you'll be hanging out over in the paying-attention-to-your-money area and then more self-value will come of it. Sometimes you'll receive value and it will wire in more self-value. Sometimes you'll give value and that process will help you value yourself more. It's a journey, folks. Dive in anywhere and just get started, even if you don't feel like you know what you're doing. There's no map or seven-step process I can give you because it will look and feel different to each person. Also, the sheer awareness that self-love, valuing your money, and giving and receiving value are important will incite changes in your life.

The most important piece of financial self-care is not what you do, it's how you do it. If you show up to your financial dates with an open heart and mind, you'll get better results than if you show up frustrated, scared, and angry. The less static you have from past resentments, frustrations, or painful financial memories in your energy field when you sit down to love your money, the better. But when you have some emotional charge come up, it doesn't mean you're a bad person or that you're doing it wrong, it simply means that there's a toxin coming up and that it's time for it to leave your experience.

CLEARING THE WAY FOR SELF-LOVE

Part 1: Seeing Self-Love

Before you jump into caring for yourself, it's important that you understand your current views of these practices. Sit down with your Money Love Journal. Do some freewriting around the following prompts:

- Self-care makes me think of . . .

- When I think about loving myself I feel . . .

- The reason I don't care for myself as well as I could is . . .

- I could love myself/value myself more by . . .

Just notice what comes up for you. This may make you really uncomfortable. It may be really fun. Notice what emotions you're feeling and where they're showing up in your body. If negative feelings surface, move your body, cry, scream into a pillow, get a hand towel and hit the wall with it for a while, go for a run, put on music and dance, journal, or talk to a friend. Whatever it takes, detox your emotional charge and then move on.

Part 2: Creating Love

Now that you've cleared out some of the emotional detritus that was blocking the path toward greater self-love, it's time to get practical. In your Money Love Journal, make a list of five ways that you can care for yourself, value yourself, and/or love yourself more this week. Here are some examples—feel free to use these and also come up with your own:

- Buy myself flowers to put on my desk.

- Sleep until I wake up on Saturday instead of setting an alarm.

- Say no to at least one person who asks me to do something for them this week (kindly and with grace, of course).

As we move through this journey toward greater and greater financial freedom together, please remember that it's simply that: a journey. This is not about getting it figured out or being perfect. It's not about making six figures in 30 days or paying off your debt in no time. It's about knowing, loving, and valuing yourself and diving deeper into your relationship with the amazing person who is you in order to create a richer, freer life.

Chapter 3

WOO-WOO
MEETS CHA-CHING

We've begun to explore our thoughts and our past regarding our relationship to money, but I want to take this one step further. There is one belief that I run into so often in my workshops that I felt it merited its own chapter: the mind-set that having or wanting money somehow makes you a less honorable or less spiritual person. Even if you don't think you feel this way, this view is so pervasive in our culture that you could experience its effects without realizing it. So, let's address this straightaway.

OUR CULTURAL MONEY HERITAGE

I met a woman named Sally at one of my Women and Wealth workshops while traveling the country on The Freedom Tour. She was beautiful and dressed in a flowing skirt. She had dreadlocks piled high on her head and wrapped in a colorful scarf. Her eyes sparkled and she had compassion oozing out of her pores. When it came time to share the things we heard about money

61

growing up she suddenly stiffened and I could feel her check out. This vibrant young woman who'd been fully present with me moments before was still there physically, but I could feel that her soul had left the building. Her eyes were glazed over and she just wasn't there.

After the workshop Sally came up to me and shared her story. She had been raised in a commune surrounded by her parents and other adults who believed that money was the root of all evil and that rich people were greedy, had cheated and manipulated their way to the top, and that anyone with money was someone not to be trusted—someone whose moral compass had gone haywire. Sally's family always struggled to make ends meet growing up and she saw how much conflict financial discussions created in the commune. There was so much negativity associated with money in her past that as an adult, Sally found herself avoiding it entirely and also re-creating the suffering around money and the lack she'd grown up with.

Her parents and the other people living in the commune were spiritual people. They practiced yoga every day, they meditated, and they studied spiritual texts as part of the philosophy of this particular community. Sally grew up to become a yoga and meditation teacher and though she had plenty of students, she never had enough money at the end of the month to pay her bills and she owed plenty of people money. She wouldn't allow herself to be prosperous because deep in her core she'd been programmed to believe that having money would make her greedy or evil.

I told Sally what I'd witnessed watching her during the Women and Wealth workshop and tears came to her eyes. "My parents always told me that money was evil.

They told me that anyone who had it or talked about it was evil. They told me never to be greedy and to always serve first, not worrying about myself. But I'm in a constant state of stress and anxiety about money because sometimes I don't know if I'm going to be able to pay for groceries. I'm terrified of charging more for my classes because I don't want to be someone who wants money. I was always taught that wanting money was bad and I'm struggling with the fact that I think of money as bad. I'm so frustrated and scared!"

Wow. Sally had a classic case of "It's not spiritual to be rich." Somehow, somewhere along the way, many of us got the memo that having money is bad, especially if you're a moral, spiritual, service-oriented person. There's a cultural meme, or thought virus, that tells us that if we want to be a good person we must sacrifice our own needs for the needs of others. But there's a fatal flaw with this way of thinking.

MONEY AND MEMES

Part 1: My Views of Money

Grab that trusty Money Love Journal of yours. It's time to go for a bit of an archeological dig. Remember, you may not think you have any negative feelings about money associated with it being dirty or unspiritual, but they may be hiding in there somewhere.

Freewrite on the prompts below. When you write something that you suspect might have something deeper underneath it, ask yourself, "What do I mean by [whatever it is you've written]?" (This is known as the "proprioceptive question" from the practice of proprioceptive writing created by Tobin Simon and Linda Metcalf.) Dive underneath your words to see what might be below. If you feel like you're going off topic, follow the thread anyway. You never know what you may unearth. It's all gold.

Address the ones that you're most drawn to and the ones you want to avoid the most first. Then go back and write on the neutral ones if you still have steam.

- When I think about rich people . . .
- People with money are . . .
- To me, money is . . .
- Growing up, I was taught that people who have money are . . .
- My experience around people who seem to be living prosperously has been . . .
- When it comes to making a lot of money I . . .
- People who live in service are . . .
- When I think about what it would be like to make more money I . . .
- In my religious upbringing, money was seen as . . .
- I've always associated money with . . .
- My current spiritual beliefs around money are . . . and the way I put them into practice is . . .
- The spiritual beliefs I was brought up with around money were . . . and the way those were put into practice was . . .

Part 2: Looking at My Views

Sometimes we journal to just get the words out, but this time I want you to go back and re-read what you've written. Circle any words or phrases that you feel emotional charge around, positive or negative. Now, answer the questions below:

- What, if anything, surprised you about how you answered the prompts?
- What, if anything, did you find when you asked yourself to dive deeper?
- What, if anything, did you learn about your money programming through this exercise?

In addition to our belief that money and greed are inseparable, we have a cultural legacy of feeling guilty for our own good fortune when comparing it to the sufferings of others. But the thing is, it is not a foregone conclusion that by your having wealth or being healthy or happy you are taking away from someone else's access to wealth, health, or happiness. In fact, you can make a much greater and more sustainable contribution to others' health, happiness, and prosperity when you have enough of these things in your own life to have surplus to give. When we sacrifice our own well-being in the hopes that our sacrifice will help someone else, we just get two people who are living sub-optimal lives.

Here's the truth: Getting sick does not help those who are suffering of illness. Being sad does nothing to pull someone out of their own depression. Becoming needy doesn't help the poverty stricken. And being hungry doesn't feed the starving. The universe simply doesn't work that way. What I mean by this is, we have a martyr archetype in our collective consciousness around being of service and helping others. It comes out in expressions like "There are starving children in Africa," said to a young child when they're not finishing the food on their plate. Yes, there are starving children in Africa, and in the U.S., and all over the world. And yes, it's good to teach children to value the food that's available to them. However, the gratitude we try to instill often goes so awry that many of us think we have to diminish our own well-being in order to help others.

If you try getting depressed enough to help a depressed person, or to assuage your guilt over being happy in the vicinity of a depressed person, all you get are two depressed people. And no one is the better for it.

Just remember, you don't have to give up your wealth or health to give others wealth and health. There's plenty of wealth and health for everyone. It's like oxygen in our atmosphere. Imagine how insane it would be to believe that we have to hold our breath because we're afraid that if we breathe deeply the person next to us won't have enough air. Similarly, sacrificing our own financial needs so that we can help someone else is misguided. It comes from a good place, but it doesn't work. (Neither does hoarding money, or any other resource, for that matter. But there's a difference between hoarding something for yourself—which also comes from a lack mentality, I might add—and simply getting your needs met.)

The truth is that you're no good to anyone unless your proverbial cup is full. This brings us back to the discussion of self-care from the last chapter. Again, you can't give someone else something you don't have. So, to be of ultimate service on the planet, fill yourself up first and then be totally generous with the overflow. True generosity can only come from a place of plenty, not from a place of sacrifice. When you're giving someone something that you don't really have the freedom to give, like money you don't have, emotional energy when you're fresh out, or even time when you're feeling pressed, you're not doing anyone any favors. The person on the receiving end will feel the constriction of that gift and whether they can articulate it or not, it won't feel right to them. And no matter how much they try to receive and be grateful, a gift given out of obligation, sacrifice, or lack that can't be given completely freely from a place of abundance can also not be completely received.

For example, let's say Jane is in a financial pickle. She asks her friend Deb if she would loan her $1,000 to help her cover her rent until she gets paid in two weeks. Deb looks at her bank balance and sees that she has $1,300 sitting in her account. She technically has the money sitting there, but she doesn't have enough to get her through the next two weeks without feeling stressed-out and constricted while waiting for Jane to pay her back. If she gives Jane money that she doesn't feel abundant enough to loan, then we suddenly have two financially stressed-out people instead of one. Deb is worried about paying all of her bills from what she has left over. Jane not only feels the inherent stress of having to ask for money to pay her rent, she also now feels the stress of owing money. Thrown on top of that is the less obvious but still very present stress that's infused into the loan because Deb didn't really have it to give. No one is the better for this particular transaction.

Consider, instead, that Jane asks for a $1,000 loan and Deb tells her, with love, that she can't loan her the money right now. Instead, she offers an hour of her time over a yummy cup of tea at their favorite cafe (total cost about $5) to help her go through her expenses and income and brainstorm some ways that she can add value over the next two weeks and increase her income by $1,000. Jane leaves the meeting with an action plan feeling totally empowered about her ability to create and receive value in the world, and Deb leaves feeling all warm and fuzzy from having had the luxury of being really present to help a friend in need. Now that's a spiritual experience.

MONEY AND SELF-SACRIFICE

Later on we'll do an exercise where you can identify financial drains in your life that are less obvious. But for now, since clarity is power, get out your Money Love Journal and list three or more experiences you've had where you sacrificed your own well-being for the well-being of someone else. We're not talking sacrifice in parent-child relationships here—clearly those little guys depend on you for their survival. We're talking friend to friend, adult to adult, employer to employee.

Do you see a common theme between your examples? Do several of your examples have to do with the same person? Do several of your examples have to do with similar scenarios? Note which people, scenarios, and parts of your life trigger you to put yourself last. Next time you find yourself hanging out with those people or in a circumstance that has triggered you in the past, simply become aware and see if you can behave differently this time. Hear my words about filling yourself up first so you can be truly generous echoing in your ears. Give yourself the same exquisite care you give to everyone else around you.

While we're talking about changing our perceptions of money, let me tell you a little story. It was September 2011. I was walking down the street in New York City after a meeting with some of the heads of Hay House. They had just offered me a contract for this very book, and while I should have been elated, for some reason, I felt awful. Walking through the doors at my hotel I ran into Louise Hay herself, the grande dame of Hay House. I told her that I'd be publishing a book with her company. She was thrilled, and I could barely muster a smile.

Realizing that my emotional reaction to this joyous news was amiss, I took myself out on a date to one of my favorite restaurants in the city. Over a delicious chocolate meringue dessert I journaled: "Why do I feel like crap after being offered a book deal by one of the best publishers on the planet?" The answer that I came up with surprised me. I knew there were people who would have done anything to get their work out into the world this way. I knew there were people who had worked their butts off and still hadn't made it. I knew there were people who had amazing, life-changing things to say who didn't have the platforms to say it yet. I knew there were people who would have been doing cartwheels on the street if they were me right now. And I felt like because they wanted it more, they should have it instead of me. I was planted firmly in the lack zone in that moment, believing that there were only so many book contracts to go around and if I took this one, I was stealing it from someone else.

God love my friend Sandra, whom I was staying with that night. When I told her my story of woe and how bad I felt about getting the publishing deal she asked me point-blank, "Kate, do you believe in abundance?"

"Yes!" I replied, "Of course! I'm apparently writing a book on it!"

"Well your thinking that you getting the chance to get your voice out there in the world in the form of a book is somehow taking that chance from someone else is insane, then. It's totally lack-mentality, zero-sum-model stuff. There's enough for everyone and your believing that you deserve this deal would be a great representation of your believing in an abundant universe, if you are in fact claiming that you do," she said pointedly.

Man! I was totally cornered. She was right. This was a great opportunity to walk my walk. Not only was I not fully receiving this gift (which stops the flow of abundance right in its tracks), I was also being self-indulgent. It was completely self-centered of me to think that I had the ability to determine what messages the world does or does not need at this particular time. I'm simply a channel for insight that needs to be communicated, and to feel guilty about having the opportunity to do so because I thought someone else deserved it more was simply depriving someone of the information in this book. (Side note: every morning before I sat down to write this book I said a prayer and asked that the wisdom that people need to hear right now on the planet come through as I type. I see myself as a receiver of what needs to be said and a translator to say it in a way people can hear. And it's a profound honor.)

Do you see how powerful our cultural influences can be—even for those of us who were raised with a belief in the abundance of the universe? For you, you may resonate with Sally's story if you experienced an upbringing that told you that money was evil. Or perhaps your own spiritual or religious community told you to give until it hurts because self-sacrifice is the path to salvation. Maybe your parents were judgmental of people living abundant lives because they were jealous so they implanted negative thoughts about having money in your little impressionable head. I am not here to change your entire belief system, but instead to simply introduce a new way of looking at things. You can take it or leave it. Just really check in with yourself as you read the rest of this chapter as we talk about the possibility that it is, in fact, possible to be spiritual and rich at the same time.

MONEY IS WHAT YOU MAKE IT

We've already talked about the fact that money is made up, just a system we put in place in order to give and receive value. So money is simply energy. The more we value ourselves and our contribution in the world, the more abundance we'll have (as long as our self-value is based on truly delivering something worthwhile that others value, too). The more we beat ourselves up and curl up into a little ball and stop shining our valuable light, the less we'll have. Because money is simply energy and we've made it up and have the ability to make more of it anytime we want (and I do mean literally— the government prints more all the time), there's plenty of it to go around.

Now, are we dealing with a situation on the planet where we could use some redistribution of money? Absolutely. But you not charging what you're worth does not feed a child in Africa. What would is if you charged what you're worth, got your finances squared away, created financial freedom for yourself, and then had the time and money to go to Africa and put in place a program that teaches women to be self-sustaining, organic farmers to feed their families from their own land like the Heifer Project does. Or if that's neither appealing nor realistic to you, once you have enough surplus in your own financial picture that you can sustainably give to others, you can contribute money to organizations like the Heifer Project, and perhaps find ways to get active in other ways closer to home, as well (personally I believe that both giving money and taking action toward helping others are important, both for us and for the receivers). Like oxygen, there's more than enough for everyone and your best bet for helping someone else out is to help yourself first.

Money is like fertilizer. It makes whatever it touches grow. So, if someone who's not such a nice person and enjoys having success at the expense of others makes money, they will continue to be the same not-so-nice person. Only now because they have more money, they have more power, and therefore their not-so-niceness expands, as does its impact on the world. Not so fun. We've certainly seen this in some of the stories of the economy crashing as CEOs walk away with millions in bonuses as their company goes down in bankruptcy and flames. Conversely, if someone who is out to change the world, to shake up the status quo, and to be of service makes a lot of money, their power for good expands. They're now able to have access to leaders who can make a bigger impact, and they're able to step into new leadership roles and take a part in making change. They are able to get their own needs fully met without worrying about them (like food, shelter, and comfort) so that their bandwidth is freed up to figure out how their gifts can be put to best use helping others.

Oprah is a great example of this. She's one of the richest women on the planet and she's changed millions and millions of lives. She wouldn't have been able to make such a huge positive impact (not to mention aid in the successful careers of thousands) if she'd stayed poor like she was brought up. A great deal of my college education was funded because Oprah had my mom on her show and tons of books were sold. That helped Oprah's ratings, it helped my mom financially, and it helped millions of women who got their hands on that book and were able to become more empowered around their physical bodies and their own wisdom. And I got a great college experience. Everyone wins when great people have money because they think in terms of, How can I be of service? And where can I help? And how can I make an impact?

MAKING YOUR NICE MONEY CASE

This exercise is especially important if you were brought up to believe that money is evil and rich people are greedy. But don't skip it even if that doesn't describe you. You can always find ways to be more loving, even if you're already one of the most caring, nurturing people you know. And that goes for your money, too.

When we've got some stinkin' thinkin' going on, it can really help to simply draw up an opposing argument to the negative thoughts that we're aware of but can't quite seem to budge on.

In your Money Love Journal, identify a limiting belief you have about money. It could be something like it's not spiritual to be rich or that all the nice guys are broke. Whatever comes to mind first is the right choice.

Now, pretend you're a lawyer in court. How could you argue against that belief? What evidence can you find to support the opposite viewpoint? What examples can you find from your own life and from the world around you? Write up the most compelling argument you can against your old, stinky belief. It's time you set it straight.

During your day when you notice that same icky-poo thought coming up, remember your inner litigator. She might be wearing a hot pencil skirt and some gorgeous Louboutin heels. And she slayed the competition in court. She had an airtight case for the viewpoint that leads to abundance, happiness, and freedom. Channel her whenever you find yourself going down the rabbit hole. She's always there for you if you simply ask her feisty little self to come on out and fight for your right to think a thought that feels better.

There's a great book my sister told me about called *It's Hard to Make a Difference When You Can't Find Your Keys: The Seven-Step Path to Becoming Truly Organized*. This book title is so genius and the concept completely applies to our financial lives, as well. How can we show up fully as passionate, service-oriented, shiny happy people if we're stressed about how we're going to pay the rent or the mortgage or put food on the table? We can't. Pure and simple. Yes, some of the greatest ideas and impulses come out of necessity, but those are mixed in with a lot of stress (which wears down on your physical health, not to mention your relationships) and an overall harried life. What we're going for here is an even, steady stream of consciousness, presence, and making a difference. And this is only possible when our own financial needs are met first. Which is why you can be spiritual and rich.

I would argue that aside from a few folks, none of us really wants money just to have money. Can you curl up with six or seven figures at night and feel like you're home in their arms? Can you call your phat bank account when you need a shoulder to cry on? No. We want money because it's a tool to get what we really want: love, acceptance, community, creative fulfillment, a sense of purpose, feeling like we're making a difference, happiness, peace of mind, comfort, and luxury, just to name a few.

If someone came to you and said that they wanted more love in their lives or a greater sense of purpose, would you tell them that those desires aren't spiritual? No, you wouldn't. You would say "Yeah, me too!" It turns out that the human condition is pretty much the human condition and within a few degrees of variance we all want pretty much the same things—and money is just a way for us to get there. How cool is that?

Obviously everyone's definition of "rich" or "wealth" is different and we'll talk more about that later. My definition of wealth is the ability to wake up every morning and do whatever I want with my time because I have enough passive/residual income to cover my living expenses. To me, wealth is choice. And my definition of rich includes great relationships, vibrant health, a deep sense of purpose and making a difference, lots of fun and pleasure in my life, and spiritual fulfillment. Yeah, having all of that is a pretty tall order, but well worth it. Interestingly enough, when I just wrote my description of "rich" I read back through it and realized it didn't include having tons of money. Fascinating stuff, this money psychology. That's because to me, money is simply a tool to create choice, the ultimate freedom in our lives. We can choose to do with it what we want—we can do evil or we can do good. Money is neither inherently good nor bad, so it's time you start looking at money for what it is. Don't let cultural ideas rule your relationship with your finances.

Chapter 4

YOU'VE GOT
YOU, BABE

Women got the right to vote in 1920. That was not that long ago. In 1975 when my grandmother was widowed at the age of 50 she couldn't even take out a loan in her own name. Can you imagine? Women couldn't get credit accounts? Is that not shocking?

I often hear women bemoan the earning gap, rant about inequality in business and the workplace, and focus on how far behind we are as a sex. When I hear that I like to remind them that given the fact that we've only been able to participate in electing our leaders for less than a hundred years, I think we're doing great.

My grandmother grew up at a time when she didn't have any other option than to get married and have a man take care of her financially. When my mom came of age in the 1960s there was still an assumption that a man was going to take care of her, if not by making all the income, at least by managing the money. When my dad came along, my mom was happy to hand over a great deal of her financial responsibilities to him.

I remember asking a close girlfriend of mine what she was excited to study during our first year of college. I looked at the class catalog and could practically feel my tail wag with enthusiasm for all the possibilities of learning. She looked back at me with a bored look on her face and told me there wasn't really anything that interested her. She wasn't excited about learning *anything* that was in there. As I poked at her trying to find out why she was even in college if a Brown University catalog didn't even spark the slightest intrigue, I realized something: she was at Brown to get her MRS degree. There we were, daughters of the women who burned their bras and cracked the glass ceiling for the freedom and possibility we enjoyed, and she had basically come to a top college to meet a guy who would be successful enough to take care of her. In other words, she was there to meet her Prince Charming.

I used to think I was above the Prince Charming trap. But in the spring of 2007, I found myself sitting in Barbara Stanny's workshop, listening to her talk about letting go of your ledge. She explained that your ledge could be the relationship you're clinging to because you don't think you can make it financially on your own, the job you hate but stay in because it's a steady paycheck, or the business partnership that just doesn't feel good but you stay in because you don't think you have what it takes to do it by yourself.

Prince Charming, or your ledge, can come in many shapes and sizes. Sometimes he's the perfect, successful entrepreneur who you imagine will come and sweep you off your feet and take care of you. Sometimes he's a Fortune 500 company where you'll climb the ladder, and in exchange it will take care of you for the rest of your life. Sometimes he's an inheritance you're waiting for to come and take care of you. And sometimes he's nameless and faceless, just a vague idea of something or someone that's going to come and save you.

Despite all of these options of what a Prince Charming, or a ledge, can be, I remember sitting in that workshop with Barbara Stanny and thinking that because I couldn't think of what my ledge could possibly be that I must not have one. Looking back I'm completely amused by my adorable oblivion. I was 24 years old living in an apartment my mother owned, not paying rent, not paying for my own health insurance, and running a business that was largely based on my mother's brand. How could I not see that my mother was my ledge? Clearly, I was so ensconced in my situation that I had no perspective on my life.

And the truth is, I just wasn't ready to let go of that ledge. In fact, I wouldn't be ready to let go of it for another four years, when we dissolved our partnership. Before that point, however, standing on the firm foundation of her brand felt grounding and safe. It felt so cozy and womb-like, in fact, that I couldn't even see how it might not be the healthiest situation for me in the long term.

The reason I tell you this is to let you know that if you can't think of the thing you're hoping will save you, or are even banking on saving you, whether it's a guy you already know or are hoping to meet, a job you already have or one you're hoping to land, or a parent, like it was in my case, it's okay. The sheer act of reading this chapter is planting the necessary seeds for your awareness to grow. Barbara Stanny helped me plant my initial seeds of awareness, and I wasn't really ready to do much about letting go of the ledge until years later. And as my dear friend and teacher Regena Thomashauer, aka Mama Gena, says, "My timing is perfect and elegant." So is yours, by the way, as I hope you began to understand in creating the heroine's version of your money love story.

WHAT'S YOUR PRINCE CHARMING?

As you've been reading you may have already thought of your thing, your stand-in for Prince Charming. Or, perhaps you don't think you have a Prince Charming you're waiting for to come and save you from yourself. But trust me, you most likely do. My mom . . . remember? So, what's yours?

Get out your Money Love Journal, and at the top of a page, write the question "Who or what am I waiting for to take care of me?" And then write out whatever comes up. Go for a page or a few. You'll know when you've hit pay dirt. You may ramble a bit but at some point something will come forward and you'll know that it's your "thing"—your Prince Charming.

BECOMING YOUR OWN PRINCE

So now you know your Prince Charming—be it your mom or your job or potential investors in your company or anything else you're hanging on to. You may be aware that it's now time to let go of that false hero and move in the direction of taking full, loving care of yourself. It's sobering how many women I've seen give away their financial power to a supposed Prince Charming, and it's just not smart. I simply must put my foot down about it. I've heard hundreds of stories over the years that have given me such a strong opinion on this. Take Bonnie's story. After 25 years of marriage where she'd worked for free as her husband's office manager, she was left with no money and no résumé when they got divorced. She didn't bother to get any sort of financial compensation or stake in the business because they were married. And she was left completely high and dry.

Then there's Stacey whose husband was an incredibly successful businessman. Besides a few acting gigs in her 20s she had never had to work in order to make money. She lived extremely well, never having to worry about a thing. Her shopping trips to Paris, her vacations to Hawaii, and her Beverly Hills home were all paid for with plenty left over. But all the while, as she was choosing not to pay attention because she figured he had it handled, her husband was investing in his brother's business. He put millions into this venture that never took off, including his daughter's college fund, without telling Stacey. When she lost him somewhat suddenly to a brain aneurism, Stacey had to simultaneously deal with the tragic loss of the love of her life and the dire financial situation she and her children were suddenly in. They had to sell the dream home they'd built and begin to scrimp and save for the first time in their lives.

These women chose to stick their heads in the sand. Let us allow their stories to be an inoculation for us to prevent the same sort of financial unconsciousness and disempowerment that breaks up families and dissolves our value of ourselves.

It's quite possible that your heart is sinking realizing that, ultimately, you have to rely on yourself for financial awareness and empowerment—that, in essence, you're the one you've been waiting for. Let me just be clear here that I am a big believer in true love. I wish the deepest, most incredible romantic love for everyone reading this book, and really everyone on the planet. However, as much as I'm a die-hard romantic, I also know the truth, and here it is: somewhere between 40 and 50 percent of marriages end in divorce and the average age of widowhood is 56 years old. So, even if you do meet Prince Charming in the form of the love of your life and he or she happens to be not only loaded, but also incredibly financially savvy, chances are pretty good that you'll spend at least some of your life on your own. And even if you meet your dream man or woman and he or she is amazing with money, has plenty of it, and outlives you, there's never a circumstance where giving all of your financial power away is a smart choice.

Do I believe in beautiful, lifelong love that nourishes both people emotionally and spiritually? Absolutely. Do I believe in receiving all of the love and adoration a man or woman has to give to you? Hell yes. Do I believe this has anything to do with being disempowered financially and opting out of financial consciousness because someone is going to do it for you? Hell no. In the best-case scenario, this sort of negligence leads to a gnawing feeling of questioning your value and not ever feeling totally empowered in your relationship. In the worst-case scenario, it leads to bankruptcy, the dissolution of relationships and families, and worse, the complete collapse of your sense of self-worth.

Remember, women only got the right to vote in 1920. So in reality we have only been valued for more than sex and making babies, or at least recognized for more than that, for less than a century. Let me repeat, we're doing great in the grand scheme of things.

That said, we still have some mythology and collective beliefs that can drag us down a bit if we don't get conscious of them. Enter Prince Charming. Most of us grew up reading fairy tales in which really good-looking equestrians rescued somewhat helpless princesses from peril. There's a cultural meme still embedded in our psyches somewhere, whether we're conscious of it or not, that someone or something will eventually come along and save us. This exercise will help you figure out, if it's not already clear, who or what your Prince Charming is. If you're already clear on this, do the exercise anyway. You'll get some valuable insight into how he/she/it shows up in your life.

MAKING YOURSELF A PRINCE

The questions below are designed to help you see what qualities you believe your Prince Charming has. It will also show you which of these qualities are also within you, even if, at the moment, they are latent. Answer each question as completely as possible and don't obsess over the answers. The first thing that pops into your head is generally the best one to go with. You'll be nicely surprised at the end by what you find and how close you already are to where you'd like to be. Remember to be completely honest with yourself here. No one is going to read this but you.

1. Go back to the Prince Charming you identified in the last exercise. What qualities does that person or that entity have that make you feel safe and taken care of? List as many of them as you can here and feel free to describe them in as much detail as you desire.

2. Look at your list of qualities you have to describe your Prince Charming. Take a pen and circle the qualities on that list that also describe you. Even if you feel like one of them could use some beefing up in you, highlight it in some way.

> 3. Choose two of the qualities you circled from your list. What is one action step you could take to enhance and nurture each of those qualities in yourself? These action steps must be specific and able to be completed within the next two weeks. Put the dates in your calendar.

If you skipped the exercises above, go back and do them now. I promise you, you won't get the results you desire from reading this book without interacting with it. You must give your money (and therefore your financial life) love and attention like your life depends on it. Because it does.

Now, go find a mirror. Or if you're reading this on the subway or in the car, just glance quickly at the window so you can see your reflection. Give yourself a nice smile. Blow yourself a kiss. Perhaps even wink. Congratulations. You've just found your Prince Charming. She's looking right back at you. You've got you, babe.

YOUR KNIGHTLY ALLIES

What is a prince without his knights by his side? Well, he's still a prince, but life is definitely better if you have help. So what do you have to help you? Your intuition. Your gut feelings. Paying attention to these nudges from the universe can really help you find the right path.

Do you remember that body bag dream I had? That was certainly an important message from my intuition. I don't think it takes a Jungian analyst to interpret this one: a part of me had died and I was trying extremely hard to make sure that no one found out about it. I was doing everything within my power to keep everything looking perfect on the outside while inside, not only was a part of me dying, it was completely dead. That was the part of me that was okay playing second fiddle to my mom in business. But it took me another year and change to consciously catch up to my psyche and realize that it was time for a major shift.

Another access point to your intuition is your feelings, both emotional and physical. For example when you begin to move toward something in your life and your body physically feels contracted and you start to feel dark emotions, pay attention. It's probably not the way to go. This is incredibly important information that can guide you toward the sweet spot where doing what you love meets being of service.

Your body is actually one of your most powerful allies. My mom wrote a book called *Women's Bodies, Women's Wisdom* that is basically a user's manual for the female body, connecting every area of our body with the area of our lives that affects it. I grew up with the understanding that our physical body is a reflection of our emotional lives. I realize for many this may be a new concept, so just take the ride with me if it is a new idea for you.

When we have physical ailments, we can connect them to an area of our lives that needs some love and attention. This mind-body connection is often discussed in relation to our chakra system, which refers to internal energy centers that are connected with different parts of our physical body (like the digestive tract, lungs, etc.) and different parts of our lives (like speaking our truth, our sense of safety and security in the world, etc.). Interestingly, the second chakra of your body, where your reproductive system hangs out, is connected with your relationship to money, sex, and/or power. So, for example, if a woman has chronic, debilitating menstrual cramps, she can look at her life in these areas. Our physical body gets out of whack to draw our attention to what's not working in our lives. We've been trained to eliminate its messages with pharmaceuticals and procedures, but if you'll listen to her, your body will always tell you the truth. She'll never steer you wrong, I promise. And given what we're looking at in this book, I want you to pay special attention to the health of your second chakra. Here's what happened to me.

Starting in the winter of 2008 I had an abnormal Pap smear and started having chronic, monthly vaginal infections. Despite trying various supplements, strict elimination diets, lots of probiotics, sitz baths, suppositories, acupuncture, over-the-counter remedies and even some prescription drugs, nothing seemed to help. Every month for about a week I would be in serious discomfort. Despite going to the doctor and talking to my mom about it, I couldn't figure out exactly what was going on, and I certainly couldn't figure out a solution.

Six months later when I went for a Pap smear it was abnormal again. This time because I had so many abnormal cells my nurse practitioner was concerned so she recommended a colposcopy where they actually scrape some cells from your cervix to have them biopsied. The whole process was incredibly uncomfortable.

Unfortunately (or fortunately, depending on how you look at it) the procedure didn't take care of everything. Instead, I continued to have abnormal Pap smears every year and fairly intense vaginal irritation every single month. Depending on my levels of stress it got better or worse each month, but there was always a low-grade discomfort.

During The Freedom Tour as I was traveling the country, living out of my car, and reinventing my entire life, my health issue got worse and worse. When I finally went to see my nurse practitioner in Maine she was very concerned with the number of abnormal cells and suggested a procedure that would remove a part of my cervix. The whole idea made me want to pass out on the spot, so I declined. She was really concerned because the abnormal cells could be precancerous. I decided not to have the procedure, choosing to channel my energy into healing my life and my body instead of simply cutting the problem out.

Six months later I was able to go in and see her again and she suggested a colposcopy just to check on everything and get a biopsy of the cells done. When the results came back she was astounded. She called me and told me that she'd never seen a healing like mine and that she wanted to begin to share my story with women in workshops she was teaching about healing cancer holistically. She said I should be very proud of myself for being able to heal this without medicine or surgery. Then she asked me what I had done. I told her I had changed pretty much every single thing in my life. She replied, "That's what it takes."

Not long after my healing, I was taking a walk with my mom in my hometown telling her about the whole journey. She offered the tidbit that cervical cancer, or abnormal cells that might eventually develop into it, are associated with the "rape archetype" of women who allow themselves to be taken advantage of. As I listened to her I felt as though a laser beam of truth was zeroed in right between my eyes. Then I got a little queasy with the next realization I had.

My first abnormal Pap smear results came back three months after going into business with my mom without a written agreement. I continued to have funky stuff going on in that area for three and a half years. Two weeks after the official end date of my mom and I being in business together, all of the abnormal cells were gone and I got the call from my nurse practitioner about my miraculous healing. In that moment I realized that those abnormal cells were trying to get my attention telling me that if I kept working in a situation where I wasn't fully valuing and honoring myself, that I was going to end up sick. It was seriously disturbing to wake up to the fact that my lack of self-value during this period of time manifested in a business relationship that began to feel squelching and was more than likely related to my physical symptoms.

It takes two to tango. As I've already said, I don't blame my mom for our business agreement that, near the end, stopped serving us both. And I sure as hell don't blame her for those abnormal cells trying to get my attention for nearly four years. I wasn't completely ready to own my power at that time so I remained in the situation until I was. And I was also not completely ready to acknowledge the connection between the situation and my health. Despite my completely holistic upbringing and my knowing that our physical bodies are simply a reflection of things gone awry in our lives, I convinced myself that this procedure would fix everything and I could go back to having a happy, healthy second chakra. And then when I finally got the message that I was enough, that I could let go of my mom as my

Prince Charming because it was time to be empowered, my cells went back to normal.

Often we go through challenges and healings in our bodies that mirror the challenges and healings that we're going through in our lives. That said, the body sometimes has its own sense of timing that may or may not be logical in relation to its correspondence with other parts of our lives. For example, after the early days of The Freedom Tour, my life was on an upswing with regard to my business and financial life improving. So it might seem counterintuitive that my health would be somewhat declining in parallel to this. However, it makes perfect sense to me. As we've discussed, my health challenge was a physical manifestation of aspects of the challenges in my business and financial life. And they'd been going on throughout the previous years while I'd been in business with my mother and living my somewhat financially dysfunctional life in New York City (even though we both know that these experiences were an important part of my journey). But my health issues did worsen somewhat on The Freedom Tour and I believe that could be because of the body's own timing. It's sort of like when a college student goes home for vacation after exams and gets the flu as soon as they get home, whereas they were relatively healthy during the past few weeks of intense work, stress, and sleep deprivation. It's as if the body is functioning under the adrenaline of the stress and then when it knows it can relax, that's when it lets go and the stress comes out in the form of the flu. The trajectory of my health situation was like that. The body's process is organic and can be part of the perfection of all of our stories.

Side note: If you have a health issue that you're concerned about, please don't read my story and think you have to change everything in your life. You probably won't have to get as extreme as I did. My soul was simply knocking rather loudly and I decided to answer her. She had an adventure in mind for me that led to tremendous healing in my physical body and also in my life. Your healing adventure may take you more deeply within, it may be more subtle, or it may even be more extreme. Your only job is to be present in your life and your body and listen for what they're both telling you.

One of the quickest and most effective ways we can get into our power around our money and, in some cases, gain insight into our physical health, as well, is to patch any energy leaks we might have in our life. If our energy is leaking into projects, people, or anything else that doesn't make us stronger, it's preventing us from being fully in our power. And luckily, money is a very practical, tangible form of energy so when we're leaking it, it's more obvious. So just listen to your body.

IDENTIFYING FINANCIAL ENERGY LEAKS

The first step of any transformational journey is to simply become aware that a change needs to take place. Rome was not built in a day, so know that this practice is about awareness, not about fixing right now.

Repeat after me: *I will use this exercise to become more self-aware, and I release the need to fix my situation right now. I trust the order of things and that through my awareness, change will come at the perfect time in the perfect way.*

So now that you're emotionally set, let's get down and dirty with our bad selves.

Take out your most recent bank statement and credit-card statement. If you have some sort of way in which you track your expenditures such as Quicken or a spreadsheet, pull that out, too.

Make a copy of each statement so that you can write on it.

Start from the top of your bank statement and look at every expense. As you read the expense and remember what it was for, notice how your body feels. Do you feel a sense of contracting or expansion in your body? If you're not sure what kind of sensation you're looking for, try this: Close your eyes and slow your breathing down. Visualize a puppy, a kitten, or a baby, or some other creature, person, or time when you felt really happy and your heart was open. That's what expansion feels like. Next, close your eyes and visualize something that generally stresses you out or makes you feel anxious. It could be a person, a circumstance, or even a sound (nails on a chalkboard, anyone?) or other sensory stimulus. Feel what it feels like in your body with this person, thing, circumstance, or sensory image in mind. This is what constriction feels like. Some people will feel this expansion or constriction in their chest, some will feel it in their solar plexus, and some will feel it lower in their gut. You may even feel it somewhere else in your body entirely.

With the expansion and contraction sensations in mind, look at each expense individually and, if possible, recall the moment when you chose to spend that money. Spend at least a moment, a full cycle of inhaling and exhaling, on each expense. Do you feel your body contract or expand? If it feels more like it did when you were visualizing a puppy, it's expanded. If it feels like it closes down and becomes tighter and darker, you contracted.

If you contracted, put a dot next to that expense. Continue until you've gone through every line from the most recent month on your bank statement, your credit-card statement, and/or your QuickBooks or spreadsheet.

Now, open to a fresh page in your Money Love Journal and write "Potential Financial Energy Leaks" at the top of the page. Then look at the first expense you marked with a dot that made you feel contracted. Write down the expense, listing the date, the amount, and what the expense was for. What is the category of that expense? Is it clothing? Is it rent? Is it food? Is it education? Is it a gift? If it was an expense that had to do with a certain person or organization, note that, too.

Whatever the larger category was, write it down in your journal, too, and write the person or organization's name next to the larger category. Repeat this process with every expense marked with a dot from your statements. Some expenses may fall into a category you've already put down, so just put a tally mark after the category that's already written down if you have a new expense that fits into that same category.

Look back over the list. Are there any categories that have more than one expense attributed to them? Are there any people or organizations that show up more than once in your list?

Are there any categories, people, or organizations that come to mind that aren't on the list that make you feel contracted when you think about them? Add them to the list.

Congratulations. You've just compiled a list of Potential Financial Energy Leaks in your life. Those expenses that make you feel contracted as you review them are not adding to your power. Your body just told you. You don't have to think too much about this. The answer isn't in your head. It's in your body. Trust her.

Now, remember, you don't have to do anything about this right now. Great job making the list. Now just leave it alone, but keep it handy because we'll revisit it in Chapter 7: Feel-Good Financial Planning.

A HAPPY FINANCIAL FUTURE

The universe has natural ebb and flow, give and take, expansion and contraction. So just as we need to move away from our external Prince Charming and realize that all the qualities we want him to have are actually within us, or that we're the only ones going all the way with us this time around, we also need to move toward something. And sometimes when it's hard to move away from something, when you're white-knuckling, holding on to something that you thought would be saving you at some undefined date, a reframe as moving toward something can help.

The only thing is that the thing I'm going to urge you to move toward is the thing that you're most afraid of. Damn, you thought you were going to get off the hook, eh? The reality is, though, that we'll never be free from fear controlling us until we saunter toward it and give it a good staredown, or at least a flirtatious wink. And the really good news is that the thing you're most scared of doing will ultimately be the highest-leverage thing you can do. What I mean by that is the amount of emotional charge you have about something that is currently manifesting as fear will be proportional to the amount of power (in increased income, success, value added, and/or sheer happiness) that is in store for you when you do that thing. A special shout-out here to Barbara Stanny who first introduced me to this perspective on resistance.

I know that many women totally space out when it comes to money, or they fall to pieces, or they just plain get anxious. I want you to know that I've been in that very spot. I pretended I had it all together for years while knowing on the inside that I didn't have a clue what was going on. I also knew deep down that I was taking actions in the exact opposite direction of getting it together. So know this: I love you right where you are. I love that part of you that thinks that money is boring. I love the part of you that thinks that money is too hard for you to understand (or to make, save, or invest). I love the part of you that would really, really, really like someone else to do this for you. I love that part of you because I have that part inside me, too. And I've learned to love her for her adorable imperfections. She comes back from time to time for a visit because lord knows this whole financial-well-being thing is a journey and I'll never be perfect at it. (Neither will you, so you might as well let yourself off the hook right now.) Do you think you're up for the same challenge? Loving ourselves in the spots where we find ourselves wrong or unlovable is total Ph.D. stuff, but given that you were smart enough to pick this book up, I'm 200 percent sure that you've got it in you.

So, let's figure out what the heck you're scared of. The reason I'm so interested in you admitting and articulating what you're most afraid of doing right now is because within that fear lies a glimmering kernel of desire, of hope, and of creation. Interestingly, in tarot, there is a type of reading in which a card is in a position called Hopes & Fears, emphasizing the fact that our hopes/desires and fears are deeply related, and sometimes they're even two sides of the same coin. Within your deepest fear lies your deepest knowing of where your brilliance would best be utilized next. And that's why you're so freaked out. There's a new horizon available to you. It's calling your name, but right now the way you're hearing it is through the lens of fear. That's okay, you're doing great.

There's a wonderful Fritz Perls quote I heard via Gail Larsen, at her Real Speaking workshops, and it goes like this: "Fear is excitement without the breath." Gold lies in the places where big emotional charge comes up for us, especially when that emotional charge comes in the form of fear. So we're simply going on a little reconnaissance expedition. We're just going to go find the fear, figure out what it's made of, what it's wearing, where it's from, who it works with, and then bring that information back to headquarters. Just like the last exercise, we don't have to fix anything or do anything right now. We're simply gathering information. Cool? Cool. Let's go.

USING YOUR FEAR

Get out your Money Love Journal and turn to a fresh new page. Fear has your panties in a jumble so it deserves the respect of a clean sheet of paper. In order to really get the intelligence on it that we need, we gotta give it some space and reverence.

Part 1: Poking Around

Complete the following sentences with the first thing that comes to your mind. Just write it down without judging it or trying to figure out what it means. The sentences don't even have to make complete sense. Consider this spelunking. Just poking around in the dark areas to figure out what's in there. That's it.

If you don't want to do this in your Money Love Journal, you can download a worksheet with the following questions from www.moneyalovestory.com/fear.

When I think about money I feel _____
_____.
Money is _____.
If I had $100,000 cash I would _____.
I feel excited about money because _____
_____.
If I didn't have to think about money I would _____
_____.
The one thing holding me back financially is _____
_____.
I feel challenged by money because _____
_____.
If money were no object I would _____
_____.
I feel like I'm adding the most value to the world
when I _____.
If I had $500,000 cash I would _____.
The time I felt most valued was _____.
If I had $1,000,000 cash I would _____
_____.
Money and I get along like _____.
What I find interesting about money is _____
_____.
What I feel scared about when it comes to money is
_____.
I really wish _____ would take care of
the money thing for me.
The most expensive thing I desire is _____
_____.
For me, money is like _____.
My mom was _____ when it came to
money.
My dad was _____ when it came to
money.
The biggest thing I worry about when it comes to
money is _____.
The one thing I've never done because of money is
_____.

Ooooooh, that was so good! You got some juicy intel. Nice work.

Part 2: Analyzing Your Thoughts

Now go back and read through your answers and answer the following questions:

1. What words or themes did I repeat in more than one of my answers?

2. What answers surprised me?

3. What answers made me sad?

4. What answers made me happy?

5. How do I feel right now right after reading through my answers?

Part 3: Identify Your *Doing* Fear

It's time to do some further synthesis of the information you just gathered on your reconnaissance mission. Since it's all fresh in your mind, might as well just dive in, right?

Now that you've started to cull some great stuff from your unconscious (and perhaps from your soul beginning to speak to you) it's time to ask yourself, what is the thing you're most afraid of *doing* right now? It doesn't have to be necessarily related directly to your financial life. But when you read that question something popped into your head. The first answer is always the best answer. Whatever you just thought of, that's it.

Take a new page of your Money Love Journal and write it down. What is the thing you're most afraid of doing right now? Don't write the reason why. Just for now, keep out the "because." The "because" matters far less than you think. You'll see. Stick with me.

Here are some examples I often hear in my workshops:
- I'm afraid of leaving my marriage.
- I'm most afraid of beginning to create art.
- I'm most afraid of taking money out of my savings account to begin investing.

- I'm most afraid of starting to blog.
- I'm most afraid of raising my rates.
- I'm most afraid of asking for a raise.
- I'm most afraid of selling my house.

Keep in mind, this is the thing you're most afraid of *doing* right now. I didn't ask what you're most afraid of in general or what you're most afraid of happening. This is a book about personal responsibility (without personal flagellation) so I want to know what you think about *doing* that you're afraid of.

Part 4: Moving into Doing

Up until this point, we've just been gaining knowledge. Getting intel. Learning about ourselves. But now it's time to do one bit of proactive work. Read your answer to the question, "What are you most afraid of doing right now?" Let's say your answer was, "I'm most afraid of leaving my current business partnership." Now it's time for ye olde reframe. Reframing this sentence to include the excitement and desire within it would look like this: I'm so excited to leave my current business partnership.

Now we can unleash the "because." The "because" mixed with your excited reframe will add ammunition to your ability to flourish. The "because" mixed with your fear just adds ammunition to your inability to act. And there's all sorts of support for adding the "because" to your fears. Let's instead add some support to your excitement.

So now add a "because" to your reframed excitement sentence and go to town. Give yourself a really good case as to why this thing you want to do is the most genius idea you've ever had. (Remember your hot tamale litigator? Give her a call.) I'm not saying you have to do it yet, but just write this next part as though you were 100 percent for sure going to do it.

What are all the great things that could happen as a result? How will you feel? Who will be thrilled and supported by your choice? What will now be possible because of you taking this action that wasn't possible before? How will you feel more free?

Brilliant! You're such a champ. I hope you're as proud of yourself as I am of you.

When I was living in NYC, feeling like a fraud, and ignoring my mounting consumer debt, the thing I was most scared of doing was leaving the safe nest of being in business with my mother and her financial support. I had a whisper of a soul calling that this would be not only a good idea, but perhaps the smartest thing I could do toward creating the life I dreamed of, but I just wasn't ready yet. It felt too big. We felt too intertwined. I didn't want to hurt her. I didn't think I had what it took to make it on my own. I didn't want to leave what felt like the security of working with her and having our financial lives intermingled.

I get that taking action toward our fears (aka our excitements) can be complicated. I get that there are moving pieces and cogs in the machines and people who will be affected by our choices. I get that it's emotional and psychological. I get all of that. And I also know that there is a perfect moment for everything to happen. *But,* there's a difference between trusting in divine timing and sitting on your ass waiting out of paralysis by analysis.

There is a fabulous African proverb: "When you pray, move your feet." Holding the entire universe on your shoulders and controlling it all is *not* your job. But taking steps forward toward what you want (even if sometimes it's masquerading as something you don't want or are afraid of) is definitely your job. If you begin taking steps, the universe will meet you more than halfway. It just has to start with you.

MAKING CHANGE HAPPEN

I recently read David Allen's *Getting Things Done*. The book is brilliant, and it totally changed my life. I could wax on, but suffice it to say, if you're looking to get organized in a really intuitive, even spiritually grounded and yet practical, way, this is the book for you. So I've become a *GTD* devotee. In the book Allen says that not identifying the next finite action step for any given project is one of our major sources of feeling overwhelmed. Once we identify and capture that step, our brain can relax and feel at peace that we've "got it" so that it doesn't have to remind us three million times a day for fear that we'll forget. Not to mention the fact that we all know that a huge project such as "write a book" or "unravel my business partnership with my mother" feels too big to handle when we think of it as a monolith like that.

When I began to realize that it was time to unravel myself financially from my mom, I didn't just do it all in one day. I was totally overwhelmed and scared, so I broke it down into bite-sized pieces. By the way, I didn't entirely know what the end result of this process would be. I just kept taking the next obvious action step until I was free. Looking back they all lined up perfectly in a step-by-step order that actually makes logical sense. But in the middle of everything I simply put one foot in front of the other and unraveled as I went. It's kind of like untangling a really delicate necklace. It's impossible to do it all at once, so you simply have to pull one strand, see where it leads, and follow it around and dislodge it from the others until suddenly there you have a detangled necklace, ready to wear.

Leaving my business relationship with my mother started with creating The Freedom Tour. At the time, it was the next finite action step I could think of. It was a sub-project of "untangling myself from my mother financially" and it felt less overwhelming and less emotionally charged. I was beginning to break my big fear, aka my big excitement, into bite-sized pieces.

After I came up with the idea of The Freedom Tour, that needed to be broken down into the next obvious finite steps. *Getting Things Done* reminds us that an action step like "get new tires on the car" isn't finite enough, so it leaves your brain spinning. Instead, the more finite next action step would be "call Mary to get the name of the tire place she recommended." A finite action step like that puts your mind at ease and allows you to actually move forward. Once I came up with The Freedom Tour, the next finite action step was to call my mother and tell her that I thought we should sell the NYC apartment I was living in. That was a finite, totally doable action step. Was I a little nervous to make this call? Yes. But was it as huge as untangling my entire financial relationship with her? No. It was doable. After that, the next action step was to call my real estate broker, then book my house cleaner to make it spotless for the photos, and so on like that. Starting to get it? Your turn!

BREAKING IT DOWN INTO BITE-SIZED PIECES

You've got your Money Love Journal and you wrote down the thing you're most afraid of/most excited to do right now. It's probably something kind of big so let's break it down together.

Start a new page entitled "Project: _____."
(Fill in the blank with an appropriate title that describes the thing you're most afraid of/excited about. For example, mine might have been called "Project: Untangle Financially from Mom.")

What is the very next, specific, finite action step you need to take in order to move toward whatever you wrote down in the previous exercise? Put a bullet point and write down your next action step under your title. If what you wrote down feels too overwhelming, you haven't gone small enough. There is always some action you can take that won't throw you completely off center. You just have to find that.

After you write the first step, just for practice, write down the very next obvious, specific, finite action step that you'll do after you've done the first one. Now write down the third action step.

It's important to note here that it's pretty likely you'll only be able to think somewhere between one and five action steps ahead at any given time. This is because things change, we get new pieces of information, and sometimes we just can't see more than a few feet ahead of us at a time. It's all good. Just write one to three action steps for now and trust that as you move toward your high-leverage thing that we identified in this chapter, the next specific, finite action steps will reveal themselves to you. No need to push or freak out. Just do the action step that's next. That's all.

You can use this framework for any fear, desire, goal, project, etc. that you have. There's something so satisfying about combining the emotional with the practical, right? And if you follow these steps, taking specific, finite, bite-sized actions toward your high-leverage thing, you'll be free before you know it. Who cares if it takes a year or even ten years? There will be magic and adventure along the way that you can't imagine now. And when you get there, the new horizon will be even more beautiful than you originally thought. And you'll be free.

Chapter 5

WHAT CAN YOU DO TO PAY ATTENTION?

I was a freshman in college. I was settling in to living away from home for the first time, being responsible for most of my expenses, and so on. I had started my USANA business that year and the seeds I planted over the summer were finally blooming. As I said, my income was above average for an 18-year-old, and before long, so were my expenses, so there was never anything much left over at the end of the month. My mom was always reminding me to sit down with our investment guy in Portland on my college vacations, but the idea of sitting there with him in his mahogany office straining my brain to understand what the heck he was talking about and what the letters and numbers R-O-T-H-I-R-A-4-0-1-K had to do with each other bored me to tears so I never went.

As you know, after moving to New York, my finances began to get a bit iffy. After a little over a year of allowing my credit-card balance to creep up a bit each month, I started to feel really ashamed. I continued to pay what I could on my balances but not pay much attention to my spending beyond that. I also began to only use my debit card instead of my credit card. I figured if I just used that I couldn't spend what I didn't have. This strategy was pretty successful except for when I came across something I *really* wanted, like a vintage Prada coat that was marked down significantly. Then I would pull my credit card out, promising myself I would pay it off in full at the end of the month.

Eventually I could no longer stand the constant, low-level anxiety that came from avoiding opening my credit-card statements, totaling up my income, and knowing what I spent every month. At this point I was not only increasing my debt every month but also going into overdraft on my checking account pretty regularly. There were several times that I had to ask my sister or a friend to lend me money until the end of the week when I got paid so that I could buy groceries and just have some cash on hand since my bank balance was overdrawn. It was totally embarrassing and I thought to myself, *Girl! You have an Ivy League education. You run a successful business. The world is your oyster. What is wrong with you?*

But all of it felt too big and overwhelming to figure out all at once. Too many numbers. Too much shame. So I made myself a promise to just check my bank account balance every morning. That was it. Just one little promise. I knew people who wrote down everything they spent and entered it into spreadsheets and totaled the categories and ran P&Ls (profit and loss statements) on their life regularly to stay on top of things. I knew people who put their money in envelopes and only spent the cash that was in each allotted category and after that, they just didn't spend anymore. I knew people who could tell me their net worth and balance-sheet data in their sleep. I was simply not one of these people (though since then I've gotten much closer to being one of them). The whole thing made me want to curl up in a corner and die, or better yet, marry a rich guy who would just take care of everything so I didn't have to. (Yep, despite my education and my exposure to powerful women, I still had that fantasy alive and well.)

But I knew that I could manage to simply check my bank balance every morning. I gave myself permission to not have it all together, to not figure it all out immediately, and to not even have to take another action step if I would just do this one thing every day. So I put a reminder in my calendar that would go off at 8:30 A.M. each day. At its prompting, I would log in to my bank and see what I had in there. Then I would give some gratitude for whatever it was, even if the balance read $34.47 and even on the days when it read -$154.59. Even on those days I would muster up some gratitude for something that felt abundant in my life—whether it was the check that was on its way to get me back in the black or the fact that I had a roof over my head and food in the fridge.

When I started checking my account balance every morning and consciously giving some gratitude for what I had or the ways in which my life felt abundant, I felt inspired to take other actions around my money. I made spreadsheets to track my expenses. I started totaling my USANA income at the end of the month so I would know how much I was making all throughout the year, not just once a year when I did my taxes. I also started working with a financial advisor who helped me start to get clear on what I had in my investment accounts, what I was making, and what I was spending. I started to realize the power of taking responsibility for and paying attention to my money. I began to unravel my "story" and realized that my actions up to that point had been relatively childish and I was sitting around waiting for someone to save me.

I had been terrified to begin to track my expenses and see where I could "shave off" some of them, as Barbara Stanny says, because I thought it would mean having to deprive myself. It was deliciously seductive to keep living in my world of buying whatever I wanted regardless of how much money I was making. There's a thrill in immediate gratification and being financially unconscious. It was my version of going out partying and making decisions I would regret in the morning. Only my hangover was receiving my credit-card statement each month and being shocked by the balance and having no clue as to how it got so high. Spending money had been my drug of choice.

But after my "aha" moment while flying the friendly skies, my resistance around tracking my money had begun to soften. In fact, by making the process fun (we'll discuss later how I did this), I actually began to love it.

At around this same time, I also had an epiphany related to the practice of tracking my money for 30 days. I had done this several times but it always felt uncomfortable, totally constricting, and just plain awful. I was never able to push through my resistance or create any positive change in my life with this exercise until I realized that I was only paying attention to my expenses.

It hadn't occurred to me to also track my income. I was only looking at one side of the equation—the side that generally causes the most stress, anxiety, and fear. When I finally did the exercise of tracking my expenses and *also* tracking my income, the pendulum slowly began to swing toward making more and spending less. I was putting loving attention on what was coming in and simultaneously paying my expenses with gratitude for the money I was able to put back into circulation.

During this time I also got back in touch with some childhood memories of enjoying being in relationship with money. I remembered the joy of counting up earnings with my sister after a day of manning our lemonade stand. I recalled how much I relished playing the banker in Monopoly and exchanging fifties for hundreds and hundreds for thousands. I got back in touch with the playful energy of paying attention to my money that I had once had but had somehow forgotten along the way. I stopped making it full of angst, fear, and boredom. I gave myself permission not to be perfect, to just take one step at a time, and to actually, God forbid, enjoy the process.

I'll never forget the day I decided on my own to meet with a financial advisor. I had met him at a networking event in New York City. He was from Maine originally, so he immediately got my attention. (Anyone from my home state gets extra brownie points.) I decided to make an appointment for a consultation with him simply as research. I got all my duckies in a row. I figured out my total investments, my annual income, my monthly expenses, and my net worth. It felt so empowering to have those numbers written down, accessible, and at the tip of my tongue. I felt strong, smart, and capable. I put on a very cute dress (purchased for only $40 at a sample sale,

I might add) and hopped on the subway to Rockefeller Center. Yep, that's where his office was.

I remembered my mom sharing her journey of transitioning from feeling afraid of and beholden to her financial team to realizing that they worked for her. She had decided to work only with people she really liked, trusted, and respected, and to never feel patronized or stupid in a financial meeting again. Armed with her words of wisdom, I rolled my shoulders back, held my head high, and sauntered into my meeting with a graceful ease.

I was thrilled that I knew the answers to all of the questions he asked me about my financial life. It was as though all the time I had spent paying attention to my money was like studying for a final exam and this meeting was where I got to put my knowledge to the test.

When he said, "Wow. I'm very impressed that you know so much about personal finance, especially at such a young age. More than 50 percent of the people who come into my office, regardless of their age, don't have a clue about most of the things we're discussing. And they certainly don't know how to relate them to their own financial lives," I knew I had aced it. I felt giddy, accomplished, and most of all, really proud of myself. I'd never felt any of these feelings in regard to money in my adult life. It was a very different feeling than the times I'd increased my income significantly or bought something I really wanted. Those were fleeting, momentary highs that felt good but didn't stick around. Walking out of his office that day I realized that money wasn't too hard for me, it wasn't boring, and paying attention to it didn't mean depriving myself. In fact, I knew there was nothing I could buy to give me that same feeling of empowerment. From that moment on, I was hooked.

PRACTICAL FINANCIAL PRACTICES

Combining the practical act of paying attention to my money with the spiritual act of feeling grateful for it was life changing for me, and it can be life changing for you, too. When people start to do one healthy thing like decreasing their alcohol intake they often report that this one action step opens the door to other small actions that cumulatively make a huge difference in their lives. Once they cut down on alcohol they suddenly have more energy in the morning to exercise. Their daily exercise inspires them to eat more vegetables because their now-healthier body is craving them. They lose ten pounds from the combination and they feel so good that they now want more muscle tone and to protect their bones, so they start to do some weight training. It's an upward spiral of the better it gets, the better it gets. And these principles apply to money just as much as they do to our physical bodies.

So let's look at some practical steps you can take that deal directly with managing your finances.

Forgive and Love Yourself

When I was in the middle of trying to eradicate my unconscious spending behaviors and get out of debt I found that one of my biggest obstacles was how I felt about myself and my behavior. I felt ashamed, pathetic, stupid, and really mad at myself for getting into debt in the first place and for not being able to stop the behavior that got me there at the drop of a hat.

The first step I had to take was to begin to have compassion for myself. I worked on finding all of the reasons why getting into $20,000 of debt was a great learning experience, and I put my attention on all the gifts it had given me. As Danielle LaPorte says, "Debt is neither good nor bad—it's how you feel about it that matters."

I also stopped making myself a bad person for getting into debt and being unconscious about my money. I finally forgave myself and felt immediately more free. And I started to love the part of myself that was scared to pay attention to her money, the part of myself that just wanted someone else to do it for her so she never had to grow up, and the part of myself that I had previously found unlovable due to overspending and getting into debt.

Practically, I did this by watching what I said to myself about my financial situation. Instead of thinking things like *You are such a screwup. What is wrong with you? How did you let this happen?* I started to think things like *It's okay, Kate. We all make mistakes and there are so many great lessons and gifts that come from any situation. You're doing the best you can and you're making progress. This situation is only temporary. You're doing great!* I decided to change my mind and open my heart to myself, and that laid the foundation for creating true freedom— financial *and* emotional. Love yourself exactly where you are, warts and all. From that place of pure acceptance you'll be able to make lasting, sustainable change.

Paying-Attention Practices

You may feel like your financial life is a total, monolithic mess that will take *forever* to get straightened out. You may feel overwhelmed, scared, ashamed, and just plain resistant to dealing with it. It's okay. But getting your life in financial order includes implementing some basic paying-attention practices. Because what you pay attention to grows. This is a simple law of the universe. Studies have shown that plants that are loved, cared for, and even sung to flourish while those that are simply watered (a baseline of attention) just do okay. Kids who have loving attention poured upon them are more confident, do better in school, and grow up to be higher-functioning human beings, whereas those who are neglected suffer in many ways. The biggest gift you can give someone is your positive, loving attention. So why not give that gift to your money?

There are plenty of people who pay *tons* of attention to their expenses, their lack of money, and their debt. And guess what grows in their lives? Yep. You guessed it. Their financial life stays exactly where it is, or even gets worse, because they're so focused on what they don't have or how much they owe. So, how do we effectively and holistically pay attention to our money?

There are many options to choose from, such as my daily balance checking. It's about choosing action steps that are quick and that can be done regularly to build up your financial consciousness tolerance baby step by baby step. Here are a number of practices you can try:

- Investing in a wallet or hand bag that makes you feel abundant. It doesn't have to be expensive. It just has to make you feel prosperous and empowered.

- Daily checking of bank account balance with a side of gratitude
- Daily expense and income tracking
- Daily money/abundance gratitude practice
- Daily money mantras (see Chapter 2)
- Daily reading of something about money (*The Wall Street Journal*, *Money* magazine, a book, etc.)
- Daily lining up of the bills in your wallet, making them face the same direction and in value order
- Weekly wallet cleanout: unwrinkle your bills, clean out receipts, etc.
- Weekly conversation about money with a buddy or your spouse
- Weekly totaling of expenses and income
- Monthly totaling of expenses and income
- Monthly gathering with an investment- or financial-consciousness group
- Monthly financial statement, bill, and account statement opening and review
- Monthly creation of a spending plan
- Monthly paying of Invoices for Blessings Already Received (aka bills—we'll talk more about this later in the book)

- Quarterly Profit and Loss (P&L) statement creation and review
- Semi-annual meetings with a financial team
- Yearly creation of financial goals
- Yearly financial review of the previous year

This is by no means an exhaustive list, so feel free to add your own that you think of now or that come to you in the process of increasing your financial consciousness.

Get Help/Support

No man or woman is an island, nor should we aspire to be. No one hands out awards for suffering through anything by doing it alone. So ask for help! This will require some humility but that's okay; admitting that we're imperfect and that we need help is good for us. Plus, it gives people around us permission to be imperfect, too. I recommend asking someone for help who is incredibly loving and is at least slightly more financially savvy than you are. They don't have to be a Wall Street CFO, but a little money know-how will go a long way. The trickiest part about this step may be telling yourself the truth about your financial situation in order to articulate it so someone can help you. It's okay. Remember, the truth will set you free. And your vulnerability and asking for help will be a huge gift to this other person. You could ask your mother, a trusted girlfriend, your husband, or a co-worker. The key characteristics this person must have are an open heart, compassion, a nonjudgmental approach to life, and unconditional love for you. And, as I said, a little financial savvy is incredibly helpful, though second to the items I just listed.

Be careful of asking people for help who are judgmental, fear-based, nagging, doubtful, or negative. This is the time to rally your cheerleaders and your supporters because your financial consciousness is just a little tender shoot right now and it needs protecting and nurturing. If you can't think of anyone to ask for help, I would recommend looking online for a local Debtors Anonymous or Underearners Anonymous meeting. These are both wonderful 12-step programs. They're free and spiritually based, and I've seen them work for many friends. You'll find people there who've been where you are and are dedicated to service. They're the perfect people to confide in and get support. (For further information about these programs focused on spiritual recovery from financial challenges, see the Resources section at the back of this book.)

If you're not in any sort of financial crisis but you'd still like to increase your financial consciousness (because, let's face it, there's always room for improvement) why not get a group together to get financially savvy with? There's something about the support and accountability of a group that multiplies our efforts and results. Plus, creating a social circle around financial consciousness will make it more fun, which will make you do it. You could read books together (like this one), commit to action steps around your money, and/or begin to learn investing together. The possibilities are endless!

Assemble Your Team

This step takes getting support one step further. Once you've found at least one person you can safely confide in about your financial life who won't judge you, get angry, or blame you, it's time to build your financial team. Here's who I recommend to get on your team:

- An accountant
- A financial planner
- An investment advisor
- A bookkeeper
- A lawyer

You won't need all of these people on your team at first, but over time as you create financial freedom, you'll likely come across scenarios where each of these people is necessary. When you're choosing people to be on your team, remember that *you* are in charge. You are choosing people who will work for you. Don't be intimidated, don't be afraid to ask them questions, and really take the time to choose wisely. For example, if you're starting a business, when choosing an accountant, ask them if they've ever had their own business before, and if so what kind. Find out how familiar they are with maximizing tax write-offs, especially if you have a virtual or home-based business. Choose someone who thinks like a business owner, not an employee. Keep in mind you don't want to hire someone who's going to simply tell you to take 50 percent of your money and send it in to the government on April 15th. This is relevant even if you are an employee yourself. There may be tax write-offs that you're not aware of, and an accountant who is oriented toward business owners is more likely to know about these than one who isn't.

When choosing a financial planner, choose someone who's fee-based as opposed to someone who works for a certain company and makes a commission from financial products that she/he recommends to you. This way you'll be sure that you're getting solid advice on which mutual funds, insurance policies, investments, and so on to make that's not influenced by them financially benefitting from selling you something specific. Again, find out if this person owns their own business and if they have a freedom mentality or a trading-hours-for-dollars/work-for-someone-else mentality. Working as an employee may be an important part of your path and/or your current financial stability, but I am interested in supporting you in creating financial freedom, and that involves a different mind-set, which we'll discuss in Chapter 8. For now, just know that in order to set yourself up for utmost support in creating financial freedom, it's most effective to work with financial professionals who have a mind-set that is in alignment with this.

When choosing all of these people, ensure that they'll be available to you for questions. I meet with my investment advisor every six months, whether I feel like I need to or not, simply because I know that paying attention to my money pays off. And building a relationship with the guy who's helping me make my money grow is part of that. I always am sure to look nice for my meetings, I ask him about his family and his life, and we really have a good time. This kind of loving, fun energy increases your ability to earn, grow, save, and give your money abundantly.

You may find that right now you don't need a book-keeper or a lawyer, but keep them in mind as you build your team. Dallas Travers, a creative career coach, often advises clients to incorporate elements in their business and career that they may not think they need yet because they should be thinking in terms of building their empire *now*, rather than waiting until it's built. It's a law of attraction thing. My mom gets together with her entire financial team once every six months to check in as part of her paying attention to her money practice. They all know one another and they all sit together to get a feel for the big picture of her company and they each report in on the smaller pieces of the whole that they're responsible for. Hooray for financial consciousness as an act of self-love!

Making Finances Fun and Pleasurable

You're only going to stick with something, especially in terms of finances, if it feels good. Yes, psychology studies show that our human instinct to avoid pain is stronger than our instinct to move toward pleasure. But creating positive, financial-consciousness habits is a long-term investment in ourselves as opposed to a momentary, instinctual decision to either move away from a hot object or move toward a piece of candy. What's great about paying loving attention to your money is that it both moves you away from pain (financial crisis) and toward pleasure (financial, emotional, and spiritual freedom). Win-win!

Whether you're currently in financial discomfort or you'd simply like to continue to expand your abundance, making your money practices fun and pleasurable will serve you. Start to associate financial consciousness with other things that bring you pleasure. For example, when I started on my financial-freedom journey, I would have a date with my money every Friday morning. I marked it on my calendar and it became "Financial-Freedom Fridays." I would clear off my desk, vacuum, put on an outfit that made me feel beautiful, put on some of my favorite music, and pour myself some sparkling water with lemon in a beautiful, hand-painted wine glass. I color-coded my spreadsheets to make the experience aesthetically pleasing. I renamed my bills folder "Invoices for Blessings Already Received." Turning my weekly financial practices into a date made me look forward to them more and stick with them. My man and I still have a financial meeting every Friday. Sometimes we do it over a nice lunch out and other times it's in our pajamas, but either way we make it a ritual of love.

My sister has even taken this a step further. She has renamed each spending category in her spending-plan spreadsheet after the goddess associated with the expense category. For example, her expenses related to the home are categorized under "Vesta," who is the goddess of hearth and home. This directly relates her financial life with her spiritual life and makes the whole experience much more fun and meaningful to her.

PUTTING PRACTICAL PRACTICES TO WORK

Let's move these ideas from theory to practice.

Forgive and Love Yourself: Take out your Money Love Journal and freewrite on some of the thoughts and judgments you make about yourself when it comes to your finances. Review the heroine version of your money story. Really just take your time to feel gratitude for where you are right now and to love yourself right there—warts and all.

Pick One Paying-Attention Practice: Review this list of paying-attention practices I outlined and see if one of them seems like a good starting place for you. Decide on one simple practice that you can commit to. The sheer act of putting one foot in front of the other and committing to taking action moves mountains and opens doorways for possibility that would never have been possible had you not had the gumption to commit. Once you decide what you're going to do, put it in your calendar with a reminder.

After your first practice has become a habit—which studies show takes about 21 days—choose another practice to add into your days. The goal is to gradually add to your practices over time. Really be conservative here and only add one thing at a time. If you're anything like me, you'll have a tendency to want to incorporate everything all at the same time and have a perfect financial life overnight. Well, let me tell you, if you do it that way you're setting yourself up for failure, just like a crash diet. Take it slow and steady. As my dear friend Danielle LaPorte says, "Everything is progress." And guess what? You're going to be in relationship with your money for the rest of your life so there's no need to move too fast.

Get Help/Support: Make a list of people in your life who you think would fit well into this support role. Remember to look for someone who won't judge you. This is the most important piece of getting help—even more important than finding someone who knows a lot about finance. Once you have the list, sit down and really think about whom you want to approach for help. Remember to use your body and your emotions as a guide. If you read their name and feel your body contract, even if in your head they seem like a good option, make sure to give some credence to your intuition. After you have fully evaluated all your options, choose one person and figure out the best way to ask for their help.

Assemble Your Team: Look back at the list of your potential team members and begin to assemble yours. If you already have an accountant you love, put their name down on your roster. If you're in search of a new bookkeeper, e-mail a few friends who are business owners to get referrals. Barbara Stanny has a great book called *Finding a Financial Advisor You Trust* with all the questions you need to ask yourself and prospective advisors to see if they're a good fit or not. You can get the book at barbarastanny.com/books/finding-a-financial-advisor-you-trust. Begin to ask around among your friends and colleagues to find out who has people on their financial team that they *love* working with. Get referrals and make appointments to interview them. Remember, you're seeing if you want them on your team so be sure to ask lots of questions and only hire the ones you feel really good about.

Make Finances Fun and Pleasurable: What do you love? Is it chocolate? Is it some really soulful R&B music? Is it the feel of satin against your skin? Make a list of things you find pleasurable and then see how many you can begin to associate with your financial-consciousness practices. If you go gaga over great stationery (like I do) then get yourself some beautiful paper and envelopes to organize your receipts and take notes on. If you love design and to create art, write up your annual financial goals and then make a beautiful poster out of them to hang on your office wall. Get out the glitter, colored markers, and stickers and make that puppy sparkle! You can even make a promise with your partner that after your weekly financial meeting you'll have a good roll in the hay to activate your second chakras.

I promise, while these actions may sound simple, and some even frivolous, they will make a huge impact on your subconscious. By making these practices fun and pleasurable, you're programming yourself to move toward doing them. Remember, how we do it is what we get. So make it fun, playful, and abundant. Give yourself permission to enjoy the process, for heaven's sake, because the journey is really all we get anyway.

LOVING YOUR NUMBERS

In addition to the practices I've outlined already in this chapter—which will help you as you move through your journey—it's important to have a good starting point. To move forward, you must get clear on where you are right now. If you want to shut the book right now and give up, I beseech you to take a deep breath, tell yourself that you love you and that you're doing great, and dive into this process in spite of your resistance. This single act of clarity and paying attention with love could change your financial life for the better forever. So for the rest of this chapter, we're going to do just that—the hard work of getting clarity.

KNOWING WHERE YOU STAND

I've created a form that will help you gain clarity about what you have and what you owe. Fill out the items below, in your Money Love Journal, or on my downloadable form at www.moneyalovestory.com/numbers. If you don't know the exact numbers but you have a pretty good ballpark figure, it's okay to estimate. If you don't have a clue what the values are here, that's okay, too. This is a great opportunity to get out your bank statements, credit-card bills, and investment-account statements to get clear. You'll feel like you can do anything once you do this. Remember, this is about loving and valuing yourself through your money. If you do this from a place of love as opposed to from a place of fear you'll lay the foundation for much more abundance in your life. Plus you'll simply have more fun doing it, which is worth it in and of itself.

NET WORTH

Assets

Value of your home:

Car value:

Bank-account balances (cash on hand):

Stocks/bonds/other investments:

Other assets:

Total Assets:

Liabilities

Amount owed on your mortgage:

Amount owed on your car:

Amount owed on student loans:

Credit-card debt (with APR%):

    Card 1:

    Card 2:

    Card 3:

Any other debts:

Total Liabilities:

Total Assets - Total Liabilities = Your Net Worth

Net Worth:

YEARLY INCOME

Yearly Income:

MONTHLY INCOME

Salary:

Commissions income:

Business income:

Gifts:

Residuals:

Investment income:

    Dividends:

    Interest:

Other income:

Monthly Income:

MONTHLY EXPENSES

Car payment:

Gas:

Mortgage:

Utilities:

    Heat:

    Water:

    Electricity:

    Phone:

    Cable:

    Internet:

    Cell Phone:

Insurance:

    Car:

    Health:

    Home:

    Renters:

    Other:

Groceries:

Travel:

    Airfare:

    Hotels:

    Bus/train/cab:

Meals out:

Clothes:

Personal care (haircuts and color, mani/pedis, waxing, etc.):

Health:

    Doctor:

    Chiropractor:

    Prescriptions:

    Vitamins:

    Personal trainer:

    Gym membership:

Gifts:

Education:

Children:

    Education:

    Extracurriculars:

Home maintenance:

    Cleaning:

    Lawn care:

    HOA dues:

Subscriptions:

Student loans:

Credit-card debt interest:

Other debt repayments:

Bank fees:

Other expense:

Other expense:

Other expense:

Other expense:

MONTHLY EXPENSES:

**Total Monthly Income – Total Monthly Expenses =
Your Monthly Cushion** or Discretionary Income, or
Basically the Money You Can Choose to Do What
You Want With (save, invest, spend, or give)

Remember as you're doing this, your Net Worth is not
the same thing as your self-worth. This number may be
smaller than you think it should be, or it may be bigger
than you thought it was. Whatever the case, it is simply
a number. Like your weight is a measure of your body's
relationship to gravity in a given moment, your net worth
is a moment in time in your money story. So just use this
number as a fact, not a judgment. It's neither good, nor
bad. It's just a number.

> This same idea should be applied to your discretionary income. If this number is negative, it's okay. The good news is that now you know you are spending more than you make. Clarity is power. In the next chapter, I'll teach you some simple ways to make that number positive that don't feel like deprivation.

Once you know where your finances stand, you can start to create a system for tracking them. This is all about organization, which is one of the best things you can do regarding your external financial practices. With information organized and with a system in place, you will be taken by surprise a lot less often. You won't look at your balance and be thrown off because you have much less money than you thought. You won't have an unexpected bill come that you won't be able to pay because you haven't factored it in. Organizing can create a dramatic change in how you interact with your money.

YOUR FINANCIAL CALENDAR

For those of you who love detail and getting things on paper, you'll love this exercise. For those of you who have experienced financial avoidance in the past, treat this exercise more like an art project. Any chance you get, bring fun and pleasure into your financial life.

Step 1: Get a calendar. If you generally pay your bills at home and you have a desk area set up, I recommend a paper wall calendar, ideally one where you can see the whole year at once. If you travel a lot or you are sometimes paying your bills at your office and sometimes at home, a digital calendar like iCal or Google Calendar will work as well. If you like working with your hands, either way I recommend getting a physical calendar to work with.

Step 2: Make a list of your bills and put each payment due date on your calendar. Even if you pay these regular monthly bills automatically, put them in the calendar with the monthly amount so you can remain conscious of what money is going out and what it's for, and so that you can take time each month to be grateful for the blessing you're paying for. For example, when I automatically pay my cell phone bill once a month, I take a moment of gratitude on the day that payment shows up in my calendar for the ability to talk to my friends, family, and business partners whenever I want, for all the fun texts that I send and receive, and for the ability to check my e-mail and surf the web wherever I am. I give thanks for the convenience and the ease with which I'm connected to the world care of my cellular service provider. See how that works?

Step 3: If you're working with a digital calendar, color-code all of your financially related activities. I recommend using orange (the color of the 2nd chakra) or red (the color of prosperity in feng shui). If you're working with a physical calendar, use colorful markers, stickers, little jewels, or anything else to add beauty, fun, and pleasure to the process. (Target has an amazing scrapbooking section with little things to bedazzle your financial calendar if you're into that sort of thing.) Anything you can do to make the process of giving value in exchange for value you've received more enjoyable will not only make it more likely that you'll stick with it, it will also attract more financial abundance to you. Remember, we attract more bees with honey than vinegar. Making your financial-awareness practices fun, pleasurable, and beautiful is about the honey.

Creating a strong container for your money by becoming a conscious and loving financial steward sends a loud and clear signal to the universe that you are ready to receive and that you'll take exquisite care of your earnings. This includes taking regular, joyful financial actions, assembling a rock-star financial freedom team, and living a financially solvent life (i.e. not spending more than you earn). When you create a strong container for your money through consistent, loving attention, you'll be able to pay off your debt (covered more in depth in the next chapter), decrease your expenses, increase your income, and increase the amount you're saving, giving, and investing. Financial consciousness is one of the surest paths to personal empowerment I've ever found. Moving through whatever resistance you may have around this is well worth it.

We earn money because we've provided someone something of value. So why not show our money we care by valuing it? By default, our self-value and self-love will expand as we treasure that which we've received in exchange for our value provided in the first place. Treat your money like it's important because it is. It is a representation of how much value you have given in the world, and so, in a way, it's a representation of you. Pay attention to it. Keep it safe. Love it and it will love you back.

Chapter 6

YOU OWE YOU

When I first started studying with Barbara Stanny and she talked about getting clear on where our money was going each month and then shaving off our expenses little by little so we had more money left over, I absolutely despised the idea. I didn't want to deprive myself. I didn't want to cut back. I didn't want to budget. I was the quintessential adolescent girl stomping my feet on my way up to my bedroom and slamming the door behind me. I was a very resistant *no* on this. I saw the value of it and it made sense to me on a purely logical level, but there was something in me that was preventing me from taking action.

In addition to my epiphany while journaling on the airplane, a contributing factor to my growth in the area of budgeting occurred through a phone session with a wonderful financial planner named Janice Goldman. She sat on the phone with me as we went through all of my financial statements to get clear on how much I had and how much I owed—kind of like we did in the last chapter. It was so scary, but with her right there on the phone with me I was able to get up the courage to just get clear. Then, she had me take a look at my expenses and see the categories where my money was going. For some of you reading this, this may seem incredibly basic to you, but I really had to start in the remedial class here. That's why I feel like I can teach this material, because I'm not naturally gifted in the taking-care-of-my-money department. I've had to work at it like developing a muscle.

Once I saw where all of my money was going (which was a humbling experience), I had the opportunity to focus on how to bring more wealth into my current financial situation. So, Janice had me start looking at where I could have some of my money go from an expenses category to a new category that she and I created called the "Money For Me" account. Every time I saved money, cut out or cut down on an expense, got a deal, or decided against buying something, that money went into the Money For Me account. This felt infinitely better than shaving off my expenses (though the result was the same) because I was adding in rather than taking out. It felt as though I was keeping more of my money, and it felt like self-care rather than deprivation. I felt motivated to increase the number in my Money For Me account so that I could use it how I wished: for paying Invoices for Blessings Already Received (aka bills), for rewarding my financial diligence with a treat, for saving, for investing, or for giving away. When I made the shift from seeing decreasing my expenses as deprivation to seeing it as keeping money for myself and taking great care of myself, everything changed.

Working with your Money For Me account will be a daily ongoing practice, and there are many ways to increase your Money For Me account as you go through your daily life. For example:

1. When you go to buy something, ask yourself if you'd really like to buy it right now, or if you'd prefer to add the amount it costs to your Money For Me account, and then make whatever decision feels the most expansive in the moment.

2. When you save money on something, like if you negotiate a lower APR (annual percentage rate) on a credit card or a lower insurance premium, you can put the amount you're saving each month in your Money For Me account.

3. When you ask for a fee to be removed from a bank or credit-card bill, you can put that amount in your Money For Me account.

4. When you start shopping at the farmer's market for vegetables instead of at Whole Foods, the amount you save on average each month can be added to your Money For Me account.

5. When you receive any sort of unexpected income, like a refund or a gift, you can put that amount in your Money For Me account.

6. When you negotiate for a higher salary, get a raise, or increase your rates, you can add the difference to your Money For Me account.

7. When you increase your business profits or decrease your business expenses, the difference in your previous monthly net profit vs. your new net profit can go in your Money For Me account.

8. When an ongoing monthly expense goes away, like when your child goes from day care (which you're paying for) to kindergarten (which is free), put the amount you were paying monthly in the Money For Me account.

The point of the Money For Me principle isn't what you do with the money. It's more about retraining yourself so that you're not feeling deprived by the idea of saving money. At the end of a week or a month, your Money For Me can be used for "necessities" like your rent, or for "goodies" like a pedicure if necessities like rent are already paid. Or you could make a payment toward credit-card debt, or put money into a cushion fund. The Money For Me principle is designed to create a way for you to feel good about spending less because it puts you in the mind-set of "that money is for me." Then you can be the one to decide what you will do with it.

One of the things that I often recommend that people do with their Money For Me account, is to start putting some of it into what I call a Surprise Fund. Putting aside 3 to 12 months of living expenses will help you out when you decide to do something like surprise your sister by hopping on a plane and showing up for her 40th birthday. It can also help you with the not-as-fun surprises, like when your kid's orthodontist tells you that your son needs braces to the tune of $3,000.

Amanda Steinberg, founder of DailyWorth.com, recommends setting aside 2 percent of your net income for this, so you don't get thrown off financial balance. This is definitely smart, but right now, let's just start by using some of your Money For Me savings. Once you get to the place where your finances have shifted even more, you can start looking at doing 2 percent of your net worth. While this Surprise Fund is essentially a savings account, starting it with funds from your Money For Me account will help you realize that the money truly is for you. It can help you do what you want. And it will help you stay sane if a bad surprise rears its ugly head.

The other benefit of using the Money for Me method of saving is that as your expenses change, you'll be conscious of where that extra money went instead of it just falling into the abyss of spending. As you get going on this, it becomes really fun to find places in your life where you can add to your Money For Me account. Keep adding ways to "find" or "capture" money to the list above.

MONEY FOR ME

Now it's your turn to create a Money For Me account. As I mentioned, this will be an ongoing practice, but we'll get it started right now. Take a look at your monthly expenses. Look at how much you've spent in each category and note the categories where most of your money goes. If there's a category that you feel is on the high side and you wish it weren't (for me it's always travel, eating out, and gifts) notice the judgment or regret that comes up as you look at it. Take a deep breath all the way into your pelvis so it expands your belly. If it helps, say the following mantra aloud or write it down:

I forgive myself for my financial past. I love the person I was when I made past financial decisions and I honor and respect that I was doing the best I could in the moment. I am profoundly grateful for all the choices in my life that have led me to this moment and my financial choices are part of that. I bless all past, present, and future financial decisions and situations as part of the ongoing creation and unfolding of my expansive, abundant, rich life.

Next, take out your Money Love Journal, and make a list of expense categories where you could take a little bit of money and move it to a Money For Me account. For example, if your eating-out expense category was $500 last month, maybe you'd like to plan to eat a few extra meals at home and put $75 in your Money For Me account.

However you do it, I recommend setting a target amount for the account, like $500 or $1000, and rewarding yourself when you get to that number with a walk on your favorite beach, a pedicure, a new book, or some other token of your love for yourself and your appreciation for this greater level of financial self-care. Remember, this reward does not have to cost you money. Quality time spent with yourself or your beloved, a special bubble bath, or reading in bed for a few hours on a Saturday are all free pleasures that can be very valuable.

BRINGING IN A BIT MORE

If you want to make more money, you simply have to give more value to other people who want to reward you by giving you money (or in some cases, it could be to just one person). It's very simple.

There are so many way to do this—from something as practical as mowing a friend's lawn to something as "out there" as getting paid to share your dreams with people. Most people even have some low-hanging fruit—these are the things you can do very easily without a lot of preparation, marketing, or other rigmarole before you are bringing money in the door. Submitting an expense report or an outstanding invoice is a great example of low-hanging fruit. I can't tell you the number of freelancers I've met who have money problems because they don't regularly submit their invoices. Hello! There are also things you can do that don't take a lot of time, such as selling some designer clothes on consignment that you don't wear anymore.

Just remember, when you're trying to add value to bring in some additional revenue, make sure what you're doing feels good and right with the truth of who you are. We've already discussed giving value vs. over-giving. Make sure the value you decide to add feels like the self-replenishing fountain rather than the sprinkler.

ADDING VALUE

In your Money Love Journal, make a list of ways that you could make money within the next 24 hours to the next month. Open your mind and write down everything you come up with—even if it's something that you currently do that adds value but that you don't get paid for right now. Write it down even if it sounds crazy—you might inspire a new idea now or later. Be sure to include really simple stuff, too, so there's an easy step you can make to launch you in the right direction.

You'll want to list at least ten items, but if you think of more write those down, too. If you're feeling really inspired or want to go for extra credit, challenge yourself to make a list of a hundred. This can feel really abundant.

> Now, go back through your list and find the low-hanging fruit. If you don't have low-hanging fruit, then look for other items on the list that might not be particularly time-consuming. Choose an item on your list that seems relatively within reach, and then, write down one practical, finite next obvious action step next to each low-hanging fruit, money-making, or value-adding item on your list. Then go do that action step.
>
> What you'll notice after doing this exercise is that your sense of what's possible will expand. And as you begin to think more in terms of how you can add immediate value to not only bring cash in the door, but also to make the world a better place, your bottom line will increase and so will your self-worth.

WRANGLING OVERSPENDING—PAST AND PRESENT

There's an adorable movie starring Isla Fisher called *Confessions of a Shopaholic* that I highly recommend watching if you've ever struggled with spending more than you make (or really if you just want a fluffy, feel-good movie). I went to see this movie in my mid-20s when it came out and was shocked by the degree that art was imitating my life. I'm not the kind of girl who's going to go for a crazy shopping spree and drop thousands on Madison Avenue for Manolo Blahniks that I can't afford, but I had my own version of this that came in the form of personal growth seminars, travel, and meals out that I didn't have the money for. Plastic came in really handy for these moments.

According to *Money* magazine, the average American household with at least one credit card owes more than

$10,000 in credit-card debt and a student graduating from a four-year undergraduate program owes an average of just under $25,000 in student loans. Given the statistics, chances are pretty good that you have some sort of debt, whether it's consumer, student, or otherwise.

Before you start feeling bad about yourself for your debt, this would be a good moment to remind you that money doesn't exist—it's just a system of value exchange. That's it. Pure and simple. So, if you have debt, you've received value and you've not given the equivalent value back to that particular party in exchange yet. That's all it means. It doesn't mean you're a bad person. It doesn't mean you're a screwup. You're not hopeless. You're not a mess. You simply have some more value to give.

If you don't have any debt, congratulations! You are living solvently, and that is a wonderful thing. Many of the principles and exercises we will be talking about in this section seem to be focused on debt, but they can also be applied to your current debt-free life. With just a slight turn, you'll see how these can help you move even more deeply into financial consciousness and well-being. They will help you gain awareness about some of the emotional issues associated with spending in general, not just past debt-incurring spending. So stick around!

Spending Shame

One of the things that stalled me out the most when I would start to pay off my credit cards and then start to use them again and go back into unconscious spending was my shame around the whole thing. I had beat myself up so much about it that I went unconscious and stopped paying attention. It felt easier to keep spending money I didn't have than to face the wrath of my inner mean girl telling me what a terrible person I was every time I tried to face reality. I was so hard on myself that I avoided situations where I would end up alone with my own guilty thoughts. This same shame spiral can happen even when you're still able to pay your bills and living within your means. Just because you're not in debt doesn't mean that you're not spending more money than you would like or on things that you don't really want or need. For me, I was in debt, and looking back on how I handled it now it's kind of hilarious that I was afraid to face the truth because I made myself feel so awful about it every time I did.

I ended up having a conversation with my friend Patty about the shame I felt regarding my spending habits and my debt, and she helped me look at things in a new way. Patty had also gotten into some debt as she launched her handbag-design business, and she had a completely different perspective on it. The way she saw it was that in order to do what she needed to do with her business, she simply had needed to borrow some money for a while. She didn't make herself wrong. She didn't beat herself up. She didn't think she was a bad person. And she didn't have any major anxiety about paying it off. Instead, she was simply taking consistent, monthly action to pay it off over time. Beyond that she didn't give it much more thought other than to be grateful for the business launch-pad she'd received care of American Express.

I do want to point out here that I'm not stating a hard-and-fast rule about incurring debt to cover business start-up costs. Patty's story is most instructive with regard to how we choose to think and feel about ourselves and our spending choices. Use your own intuition when it comes to deciding whether or not to spend a great deal or even incur debt, for business or personal reasons. It's crucial, though, to be extremely conscious when making these financial decisions. Just as different people have different physical constitutions and metabolisms and therefore respond to different foods in different ways, we all have our own particular financial constitution. It's important to know your own well enough to know whether or not it's safe for you to deplete a good chunk of your savings or incur well-considered debt. For some people incurring debt of any kind is just a slippery slope. If you're not sure if this is a good idea, just take a look at your history with debt, and if you're still not sure, check out some Debtors Anonymous meetings and notice how much you identify, what resonates, and how much resistance comes up—all useful information and clues.

That said, talking to Patty about her perspective on debt was revelatory for me. For the first time I realized that there was another option other than feeling like crap about myself for it. When we dislike a situation we're in, or when we deem ourselves or other people to be wrong, it's nearly impossible to move forward and transform. Beating ourselves up or complaining about something or someone is like digging a hole deeper right under our feet to get us more entrenched in whatever situation, relationship, or personal struggle we're facing. I realized that by feeling guilty, ashamed, and embarrassed about what I had spent and what I was spending I was not only preventing myself from taking a solid, truthful look at it, but also keeping myself firmly planted in debt. This is true any time we let ourselves stay entrenched in shame, whatever the issue may be. It can be a very paralyzing emotion.

FREE ASSOCIATION ON FINANCIAL SHAME

Take out a fresh page in your Money Love Journal, set a timer for 20 minutes, light a candle, put on some classical music, and freewrite on your debt. If you don't have debt, but feel that you don't really have your spending under control, write on that. If you don't have a source of financial shame, feel free to skip this exercise, but be honest with yourself; don't just gloss over it because you don't feel like doing it. This can be a very healing exercise.

Allow yourself to write down anything that comes to mind and try to not lift the pen from the page; just fluently write exactly what comes into your mind on the paper. It doesn't have to make sense, have perfect spelling, or have correct grammar. Don't censor yourself. If you need some inspiration, ask yourself the following questions:

1. What does being in debt or out of control of my spending mean to me?

2. How does it feel to be in debt or constantly out of control in my spending?

3. Why did I end up here?

4. How do I feel about myself when I think about my debt or spending habits?

5. What does my debt or spending represent?

When you're done, read back over your writing and highlight or circle anything that jumps out at you as surprising, profound, or disturbing. Also note anything that's a new insight you've never had before. Awareness is the first step to unraveling and changing our relationship with money. Opening your eyes to the way you feel, the thoughts you think, and the way you talk to yourself when it comes to debt and spending is incredibly helpful to bring more awareness.

INVOICES FOR BLESSINGS ALREADY RECEIVED

As I've already said, I like to call bills Invoices for Blessings Already Received, or IBARs. Full disclosure: I didn't make up this terminology. A number of other teachers of prosperity consciousness (including Randy Gage) use it, and I'm not sure exactly where it originated, but I love it. This designation immediately removes negative emotional charge and puts me in a place of gratitude for what I have in my life as a result of my spending decisions. I recommend you rename your debt balances and bills IBARs or create your own creative name that feels good. Words are powerful because they elicit certain emotional responses in us that lead us to take certain actions that lead to certain results in our lives. Please do not underestimate the importance of choosing the words we use. From here on out in this chapter, debt will be referred to as Invoices for Blessings Already Received. I feel lighter already. Don't you?

The goal of this section is to get into agreement with your spending. We've already worked on not feeling shame about debt or overspending. Now it's time to go even further—to feel gratitude for what this has given us.

INVENTORY OF INVOICES FOR BLESSINGS ALREADY RECEIVED

Step 1: Inventory of Your Invoices

Before we can get into agreement with our current situation, we first have to know exactly what our current situation is. So now it's time to do the fabulous IBAR inventory. If you need to put on some red lipstick or a favorite song or pour yourself a delicious beverage in order to psych yourself up for this, do so now. Any or all of those activities just enhance the exercise, in my opinion.

Get out all of your most recent credit card, student loan, car loan, mortgage, home equity loan, or any other type of debt or loan statements. If you owe a friend or family member money, write that up on paper, too. Don't leave anything out. It's time to put it all down in black and white. In your Money Love Journal title a blank page Inventory of My Invoices for Blessings Already Received, or you can work with the free IBAR Inventory Handout which you can download at www.moneyalovestory.com/IBAR.

Be sure to take deep breaths down into your belly as you do this. I recommend putting on some fun music and doing a dance break during this exercise or right after to celebrate your clarity and your willingness to tell yourself the truth. (If you need song ideas, visit www.moneyalovestory.com/playlist for my Money Love playlist.) This is not necessarily easy stuff, but taking these little steps can lead to huge transformation. But first you have to start right where you are. Note that much of the information you'll need for your IBAR Inventory is already listed in the Loving Your Numbers exercise we did in Chapter 5. Listing this information separately from the Loving Your Numbers exercise is often important for people because debt and overspending can be such emotional issues. So, let's go!

Start by looking through your spending. For those of you who are in debt, here are a few steps specific to you:

- Make a list of all the people or organizations you owe money to. These are your givers.

- Next to each giver write down how much you owe them.

- Next to each amount owed write down the interest rate (APR) if there is one.

- Next to each interest rate write down the minimum monthly payment if there is one.

- Next to each minimum payment write down the payment due date if there is one.

For those of you who are not in debt, but are just dealing with out-of-control spending, make a list of those purchases that make you feel shame. This is similar to what you did when you were finding potential financial energy leaks in Chapter 4, but this time, we're doing it with all of your expenses.

Nice job! Repeat after me: Clarity is power. Clarity is power. Clarity is power. It might be painful to face your IBARs, but trust me, getting clarity and being willing to look at it square in the eye will move you forward faster than avoidance will. Congratulations for going there. I'm proud of you and you should be, too. It's a huge step.

Step 2: Inventory of Your Blessings

This next step is so fun. Now that you've got your IBARs all clear and organized and you know what you owe, to whom, and by when, it's time to recall all of the blessings you've received already as a result of your spending. Take your car loan, for example. You've likely traveled thousands of miles in your car and had the opportunity to do tons of things you would not have gotten the chance to do if you didn't have your fine set of wheels. This step is about taking inventory of all the ways your life is better because of the debt you've incurred or the overspending you've done.

Next to each giver or shame-inducing expense on your IBAR Inventory list, write a list of things you're grateful for that came into your life as a result of that particular expenditure. Write down the physical items you bought and how you enjoyed them. Recall the people you met on the trips you took. Take note of all of the incredible memories you've experienced in your home. Take a moment to appreciate what you learned from the classes you enrolled in. Notice all of the ways your life has been enhanced through the value you've received from your various spending choices. Take as much time as you need on this step as it may be the most important one you do in your debt-clearing journey. Make sure to take deep breaths and allow yourself to indulge in the experience of recalling positive memories from your past.

How does that feel? Isn't it amazing what a reframe can do? When I started renaming my bills folder "Invoices for Blessings Already Received" and paying my debt from a place of gratitude and an equal value exchange, things in my life shifted dramatically. My income increased, and so did the rate at which I was decreasing my debt and spending. I was able to stop incurring debt for the first time since I had started (despite having tried many times before) and I felt better about myself. The seemingly minute inner steps we take that move us more toward love, gratitude, and appreciation create seismic shifts in our exterior world.

There's no amount of feeling guilty and ashamed about your debt or overspending that will make it disappear. And, when you take action steps from the place of fear, guilt, anger, lack, or shame, your results won't get traction in the same way they will if you're able to find the place of love and gratitude within yourself. I'm not suggesting that this shift happens overnight, but consciously putting your attention on changing your mind about what your debt and overspending mean is a very worthwhile endeavor. The action steps taken with a positive mind-set toward paying off your debt or reining in your spending will be easier to stick with and will have a more profound, sustainable impact on your financial situation.

EMOTION AND DEBT

Let's move on to something that is solely for those readers who are in debt. While those of you who aren't may find this eye-opening, feel free to skip this section.

So, let's say you're in debt. You've started the process of getting your head screwed on straight about your debt and you're no longer digging yourself deeper by feeling bad about yourself and your situation. Now it's time to create a plan to get to zero debt. I agree with my friend Patty that debt doesn't mean you're a bad person and that you don't need to make paying it off the most important, all-consuming, totally stressful focus of your life. However, there is something about knowing that you owe someone something that can throw off the balance of your creative juices. As I said earlier, a debt simply means you've received value for something and you've not yet reciprocated that value. No big deal. You just want to set the balance straight.

I love Adam and Courtney Baker's approach to deciding which debt to pay off first. You can read more about their work at www.manvsdebt.com, the fabulous personal-finance blog that Adam created about living a life of financial consciousness and freedom. (Adam's wife, Courtney, now runs the site.) What most approaches to paying off debt are missing is the emotional piece. Since we made the whole money system up, what has value is completely subjective. It's also emotional. We make all spending decisions from our limbic brain, which controls our emotions, and then we justify them with our frontal cortex, the logical part of our brain. But as much as the men in suits want us to believe that value is inherent in certain things and therefore finance is a logical endeavor, they're just wrong. Value, money, and the economy are completely wrapped up in and dependent upon human behavior, and therefore human emotions.

So when a debt repayment strategy doesn't take into account how we feel about our debt, it's completely missing the mark. What I love about the Bakers' strategy is that it brings our emotional experience front and center. Other strategies I've come across suggest paying off the debt with the highest APR first or paying off the card with the lowest balance first to give yourself a sense of completion and progress. The Bakers, on the other hand, suggest paying off the debt that has the most negative emotional charge first. For example, if you owe $5,000 to your parents and it has no interest rate on it, but every time you talk to them or see them you feel incredibly guilty, that one is negatively affecting your life *way* more than the 15 percent–interest credit card that you pay off dutifully a little bit every month but has no emotional charge attached to it. Get it? It's a super-smart approach and very intuitive, if you ask me. I suggest keeping this principle in mind when making important financial decisions even if you're not in debt. Divorcing our emotions from our money is not a good idea because it's basically just denial. We don't want to let our emotions take over completely, but they do deserve a degree of respect as an important part of the equation.

RANKING EMOTIONAL DEBT

Take a look at your list of Invoices for Blessings Already Received. Next to each one, mark down an "Emotional Impact" rating from 1–10, with 1 representing an invoice that has little to no emotional impact on you, and 10 being an invoice that you think about constantly and has a great deal of emotional charge that comes along with it. Common emotions that might create this charge are shame, guilt, resentment, fear, or anger.

> Now, make a new list of your Invoices for Blessings Already Received with the invoices connected with the highest emotional charge at the top and the lowest at the bottom. This is the new order in which you'll pay off all your debt. With each payment you will gain more and more emotional freedom and feel lighter and lighter!

So there you have it—a general structure for how you can pay off your debt—and then it's time to make a plan, Stan. You know how much you owe, to whom, by when, with what interest rate, and how much each debt is affecting you emotionally. Since paying off debt is personal to each situation, you have to take it from here. But remember, from an energetic perspective, we don't want to focus too much on our debt. Instead, we want to pay enough attention to it to know it's there, to acknowledge its effect on us, to have some gratitude for what we've received in exchange for it. And then simply put a plan in place to get it paid off. This plan may include increasing your income through adding more value and/or decreasing your spending through adding to the Money For Me account and paying your debt from the increase. It's up to you what balance of these two sides of the coin works for you.

A word of caution for those paying off debt: When I was paying off my debt I sometimes would get overly enthusiastic because it felt so good to see the numbers on my credit card statements go down. But my enthusiasm would sometimes result in going into overdraft on my bank account, which was basically creating more debt. So, I urge you to be methodical and have an "easy does it" mentality around your debt payment. Choose an amount to pay off each month that feels spacious and won't require you to scramble and scrimp. One suggestion I've heard for people coming out of a cycle of debting (especially if they also have a history of underearning or are doing so presently) is to allot a maximum total of 3 to 5 percent of your monthly income toward debt repayment. This means that all of your payments to all creditors would together add up to no more than 3 to 5 percent of your income. Paying off your debt is an opportunity to infuse your life with a feeling of abundance. And the quickest route to abundance is consciousness, not rushing.

When creating a plan to pay off your debt, start from the place of looking at your financial cushion—the amount of money you have left over (or not left over) after you pay all of your necessary expenses each month.

Your monthly cushion may be a positive number or a negative number. In the spirit of financial awareness as a profound act of self-care, we want to plump up that cushion so that it's plush, luxurious, and a soft place to land that you've created for yourself. This can be done by diverting a bit of your money from your Money For Me account or by finding a way to bring in more income. Or it can be done by finding a way to reduce your expenses. When framed as taking great care of yourself, it becomes far easier and more pleasurable to stay consistent with any changes you make. Don't worry if your cushion is a negative number right now. If you follow the guidance in this book that number will be positive in no time.

Your monthly cushion is the money you have available to you to pay down your debt.

USING YOUR MONTHLY CUSHION

At this point, it's time to figure out the amount of your monthly cushion and how to use it to cut down your debt. So first, open up your Money Love Journal and revisit the figures you found in the Loving Your Numbers exercise. Then set up a simple subtraction problem:

Total monthly income – total monthly expenses = monthly cushion

If your monthly cushion is a positive number, figure out how much of that number you'd like to put toward paying your debt each month. Decide on a number that meets your minimum payment at the very least (but ideally is more) and that feels spacious, comfortable, and doable. Remember to keep it small enough that you don't go into deprivation. Be sure to infuse your life with the things you value, too, like the occasional meal out or a pedicure from time to time. This is not about living life like a monk. It's about slowly, steadily, and elegantly giving value in exchange for what you've already received. As you increase your Money For Me account, you may be able to increase this number bit by bit every month or pay off an extra chunk from unexpected new income or by significantly decreasing another expense.

Once you have this amount figured out, write it down. From there, you'll want to divide this payment into the different categories of your various IBARs, paying the highest percentage of it to the IBAR you determined had the most emotional charge in the Ranking Emotional Debt exercise.

If your monthly cushion is a negative number, it's time to go back and look for some ways that you can fatten that cushion by increasing your income or decreasing your expenses. Ask yourself, where can I add more value to the world? Also ask yourself, what expense areas can I reduce to create a more abundant cushion for myself? This is about loving yourself, not depriving yourself.

In addition to the financial calendar that you set up in the previous chapter and your repayment plan for blessings already received that you set up in this chapter, I recommend setting up some sort of additional tracking system so that you can enjoy the process of seeing your credit card and other loan balances go down. Studies show that the simple act of tracking our progress can have a profound impact on improving the number we're tracking. People often lose weight simply by tracking their weight every day on a chart without making any dietary or exercise changes. Imagine the impact you can make by tracking *and* taking action!

Maybe you'd like to make a big chart and hang it on your wall and mark your progress on a line graph. Maybe a spreadsheet in your computer would work well for you. Whatever it is, you'll be more likely to stick with it if you have some way of tracking your progress and visually seeing your success. Every payment counts and is worth celebrating. This could also be helpful and empowering as part of a savings or investing strategy. If you set a savings goal or a goal for investing a certain amount of money in a Roth IRA, for example, tracking your progress carefully will be quite motivating.

LIVING A JOYFUL LIFE—EVEN WITH DEBT OR OVERSPENDING HABITS

It turns out our lives are happening right now. I used to feel like somehow I couldn't start enjoying myself or being proud of my other successes in life until my debt was paid off. I let the guilt and heaviness of my debt weigh me down and prevent me from being fully present in the moment. And all I was doing was punishing myself. When I forgave myself and stopped making the debt make me into a bad person, I gave myself permission to relish my successes while knowing that my debt was shrinking every day.

Please don't hold off on living your life with abundance and joy because you owe some value in exchange for blessings you've already received, or because you haven't met a particular financial goal. Your enjoyment of life is one of the ways you add value to the planet and you stifling it only adds more debt and deprivation to your life on an energetic level. Instead, find ways to create abundance daily. Enjoy nature. Laugh with your kids. Eat slowly and savor every bite. Make love. Watch funny movies. Do things that make you feel alive. It's possible to live abundantly without spending a lot of money and the more you enjoy every freaking moment of your life, the more value you'll be adding to the world, and the faster you'll be able to pay off those Invoices for Blessings Already Received and create more prosperity in every area of your life, both financial and otherwise.

Chapter 7

FEEL-GOOD FINANCIAL PLANNING

The 2008 economic crash was caused by people, businesses, and governments spending beyond their means. Plain and simple. My hypothesis, which we'll spend this chapter diving into, exploring, and backing up on a more philosophical level than scientific, is that most of the time when we're spending beyond our means, we're buying things that aren't in true alignment with our values.

For example, when I got myself into debt, most of the things I bought that I didn't have the money for were things that would make me look or feel a certain way that I felt I couldn't look or feel without those things. Some of the things were solid investments in my business and growth that were well worth it. But the unconscious ones were more often than not out of alignment with my values. I'm not proud of this, but I'm peeling back this particular layer of the truth onion so that you feel safer to dive really deep, too. I bought dresses and shoes to look professional, affluent, beautiful, and sexy. I paid for seminars because I thought the teachers had access to a special wisdom that I wouldn't have access to unless I went to their event. I took trips that I didn't want to say no to because I wanted to hang with really successful people and look as though I was one of them, even though I was paying for it on my credit card.

I'm not going to lie. Writing that last paragraph makes my stomach turn. Admitting to myself (and to you) that most of my overspending came from wanting to look more successful or more together than I actually was is like standing naked in front of an audience of thousands. It may even be worse than that. But I once had a great coach named Rebecca Bent who said to me, "Your truth changes people's lives." So I stand here naked in front of you in the hopes that you'll be willing to shed your outer layers as well, and reveal the core of your financial woe, past or present, at least to yourself and hopefully to at least one other human being.

I first strengthened my self-worth by using money as a tool for self-love, becoming a more vigilant steward of my money, and noticing how abundant my life already was without needing to buy stuff to make it more so. I then stopped feeling as though I needed to spend money I didn't have on things that would make me look a certain way to others. Again, I would venture to say that most financial decisions that cause people, businesses, and governments to spend beyond their means (which is a way of throwing themselves under the bus) are not in alignment with the true, core values of these people or organizations, but instead, are coming from a place of wanting to look or feel a certain way stemming from a fundamental lack of self-worth.

We're getting into the deep, murky stuff here. If you're recognizing a hint of truth in these words for yourself, congratulations. Diving deep into the muck is what allows us to flourish on the other side. Seeds are sprouted in the dark with the help of fertilizer or organic material in the earth. And you know what organic material in the earth is made of? Animal and plant decay and excrement. Yucky, dark, mucky crap, basically. It's the substrate of all natural beauty: rose gardens, redwoods, the lily pads in Monet's garden, and the sweet-smelling beach grass on the shore. The deeper you're willing to go in your honesty and transparency about your values and your financial decisions, the higher you'll be able to fly and the sweeter your life will be.

HAVING WHAT WE WANT
INSTEAD OF HAVING IT ALL

Marketing campaigns touting the wonders of modern society tell us that we can have it all. But the truth is, nobody actually wants it all. We're all incredibly unique creatures and what makes one person tick makes another person tock. We really only want what we want. Philosophical and positive psychology wisdom tells us that happiness comes from wanting what we have instead of having what we want. I'm totally down with this. I've kept a gratitude journal for years. Every night before we go to sleep my man and I each share three things we're grateful for. Practicing appreciating what we already have is one of the fastest roads to fulfillment.

However, I think it's possible to *both* have what we want *and* want what we don't yet have. Let's join the *both/ and* party instead of the *either/or* party, shall we? Thinking inclusively and in possibilities is the bedrock of an abundance mind-set. And guess what? An abundance mind-set creates abundance in our lives. Let's change from "It's not possible," to "How can it be possible?"

So, if we want to have what we want *and* want what we have, we've got to first figure out what it is that we want. This is not such a simple question. I can't tell you how many people I've worked with personally who've never taken the time to actually get clear on what they want, what they value, and what brings them joy. Because when you're defaulting on your student loans and are afraid you're not going to be able to cover the rent, who has time to ask silly questions like "What brings me the greatest joy and fulfillment in life?" or "What do I truly want?" Is getting to ask yourself these questions a luxury? Absolutely. But guess what, it's free! And getting yourself into alignment with what truly turns you on lights up the whole world.

A rich life looks and feels completely different to different people. A friend of mine just spent his vacation packing up everything he would need for a week in the woods, driving 14 hours to the boundary waters in northern Wisconsin, and canoeing and hiking for six days, many of which were in the rain. He was ecstatic to do this. To me it sounded miserable, and I was simply thrilled to look at the pictures while freshly showered and dry.

My dad loves to study literature. He goes crazy for the classics. At the age of 65 he's still enrolling in literature classes because he just can't get enough. Most of the classics (save some really great Austen novels and a few others) make me want to take a snooze, but they really do it for him.

I know a CEO who relishes jumping out of planes for fun and a high school teacher who lives in a tiny apartment with her giant cat Small and adores knitting. Different strokes for different folks. The quilt of human desire, value, and joy—so abundant, so rich, so multidimensional. The beauty of being human is that we're all so different. So now it's time to find out who you are so you can better align your financial life with your true self.

DEFINING YOUR RICHES

Since everyone has a different definition of riches or wealth, it's time to craft yours. Let's start with a brainstorm. Open your Money Love Journal and list ten words or phrases that come to you when you hear the words *riches* and *wealth*.

Once you're done, circle or highlight the words that really resonate deeply. If it's all of them, circle them all. This exercise is about abundance so you don't have to limit yourself.

Now, organize your words and phrases into a definition. You can choose *wealth, rich, riches, abundance,* or any other word that feels like it really resonates when it comes to pinpointing the quality you'd like to have in your life associated with financial well-being and having enough or more than enough.

In your journal, simply write: "My definition of _____ (your word goes here—*riches* or *wealth* is a good place to start) is" and then start defining.

Read over what you've written. This is what you need in your life to feel wealthy or rich or abundant. Congratulations! You've just taken your first step to values-based financial planning.

Out of interest, I asked my Facebook community for their definition of *riches* or *wealth*. Here are some of the answers:

- Having a community/tribe that never fails to rock my world every day.

- Wealth is the love and support of family and friends, which makes for the riches in life.

- Having Inner Peace.

- Having the freedom and creativity to do whatever my heart desires.

- Wealth: The state of inner fulfillment that frees you to give to others unconditionally.

- Health + happiness + inner peace + freedom + hugs + nice electric guitars . . . hee! :)

- Financial wealth for me: to always be able to choose the best alternative without having to let the price tag speak.

- Wealth = wanting/savoring/appreciating what you have, regardless of the category (love, work, adventure, chocolate, etc.)

- Wealth is being able to say, "I have everything I need," and mean it. It's being able to do what you want, when you want, in the company of those you adore. It is freedom to discover who you REALLY are, and to act in service.

- Ease. Letting the worry slip away replaced by dreams.

One woman wrote in and noticed that when we define wealth we often leave out the financial part of the picture. We shy away from including money because we think we shouldn't want it or that it's not okay to even talk about it. Another then wrote in and asked, wouldn't we rather be poor or middle-class and enjoy our health than have money? The first woman responded, why do we have to choose? I agreed.

Defining wealth on our own terms doesn't mean leaving money out of the picture. That's just a bypass and avoidance in a different dress. But it also doesn't mean making it only about the money and forgetting why we want money in the first place.

What I love about defining riches and wealth for ourselves is that we get to create them on our own terms. We don't have to do it the way our parents or grandparents or ancestors before them did it. We don't have to do it the way our best friend or our co-worker does it. When you get clear on your own definition, the only person you have to please is you. And let me tell you, it's such a relief to give up trying to make other people happy. You're the only one who has to approve of your life. So now, you just have to figure out what types of possessions, environments, and experiences will bring you the most satisfaction. Money doesn't buy happiness, but it certainly makes life more pleasant.

PEAK MOMENTS

Think of three times in your life that you felt your best. These times were full of joy, feelings of expansiveness, and any other positive emotions that you recall. Examples might be the day you gave birth to your first child, a fantastic trip you took to a beautiful country, or a simple afternoon reading a great book by the fire. There are no wrong answers. Please don't spend too much time trying to think of the "right" or "best" moments; the first three that come into your head are most likely the best ones to work with.

In your Money Love Journal, write down the three peak moments. Describe them in as much detail as you can remember. What were you doing? Who were you with? What do you remember seeing, hearing, smelling, and touching? Where were you? How did you feel? What were the circumstances surrounding this experience? What made it memorable?

Once you've written down everything you can possibly recall from these experiences, go back and read each one. If you have someone you can do this exercise with, even better. Read through your descriptions to that person and ask them to listen for common themes in all three. Whether you're doing this exercise alone or with a partner, after reading your peak moments aloud, make a list of common themes throughout all three experiences. For example, you may have noted that in all three moments you were surrounded by the people you love most. Perhaps in all three you were outside in nature. Or maybe they all involved travel, adventure, or accomplishment. Whatever the common themes are, write them down.

The first time I did an exercise like this—which is actually what inspired me to include it—it was being led by Andrea Scher and Jen Lemen, founders of the Mondo Beyondo online course (www.mondobeyondo.org) at the

World Domination Summit. The work I did with them really helped me home in on what I value most in the world, on what is most important to me. And the Peak Moments exercise above can do the same for you. If all three of your peak moments involve being in community with people you love, you can be pretty sure that that's of high value for you. If they all involved being recognized for achievement, then that's a high value for you. Please don't second-guess or judge this list. This is simply information about yourself and it's wonderful. You're the only one going all the way from birth to death with you this time around, so you may as well take the time to compassionately get to know you.

The next thing we're going to do is look a little more deeply into the common themes of these peak experiences. You've identified the commonalities between the circumstances surrounding your experiences, now it's time to see what these represent for you. What values do these bring to your life?

WHAT DO YOU VALUE?

Take the list of common themes from the Peak Moments exercise and next to each one, write what value it represents for you. For example, if a common theme in all of your experiences is being surrounded by the people you love, that could represent your values of love and community, so you would write those next to that item on your list. If you have *recognition* on your list of common themes, then that's one of your values and no change to that word is necessary. If you need some examples of values, check out the list below. This list is in no way exhaustive so feel free to add your own.

abundance	entertainment	love
achievement	excitement	loyalty
adventure	expansion	nature
beauty	family	openness
belonging	freedom	peace
commitment	friendship	pleasure
community	fun	possibility
companionship	generosity	purposefulness
connection	gratitude	recognition
consciousness	health	relaxation
conservation	humor	safety
contemplation	innovation	security
contribution	integrity	service
creativity	joy	solitude
ease	kindness	spirituality
embodiment	laughter	sustainability

Now, take the list of values that you wrote next to the common themes from your peak moments and pick the top four or five that most deeply resonate with you. These are the words that most describe who you are and what's important to you.

Wasn't that clarifying? There's something about drilling down to some key aspects of who we are that is incredibly freeing. It gives us a firm foundation in a world of limitless choices. Hold on to this. We'll come back to it.

ATTRACTING WHAT YOU WANT

When I was in high school my mom taught me a really important tool for manifesting good things into my life. She told me that if I can hold pure, positive energy in my thoughts and emotions for 17 seconds it puts out a clear vibration so that I can manifest what I want. She had learned this concept from the work of Abraham-Hicks (www.abraham-hicks.com) and their teachings about the law of attraction. Listening to their work and then expanding my research to include other metaphysics teachers taught me that in order to manifest what we want, we need to focus on feeling good. When we focus on feeling good instead of manifesting a specific red sports car, then we attract experiences that make us feel good. One of those experiences may be having a red sports car, or it may not. The point is, none of us wants things in life because we actually want the things. We want certain things because we want to feel a certain way. And the great thing about focusing on how we want to feel instead of what we actually want is that we'll be pleased by what we manifest in our lives instead of having our claws digging into the way it has to be in order for us to be happy. Your subconscious and the universe are far more creative and wise than you often give them credit for. Focus on how you want to feel, organize your life to feel that way more often, and then sit back and watch how it all comes to pass majestically unfold.

Danielle LaPorte does a great job articulating the idea of focusing on feelings rather than what we want, and guiding us through ways to apply this to our lives with her concept of "core desired feelings" in her program *The Desire Map* (she also touches on it briefly in *The Fire Starter Sessions*). I highly recommend getting her program to dive more deeply into defining how you want to feel as a compass for creating your life. (You can find a link to *The Desire Map* program in the Resources section at the back of this book.) This next exercise is inspired by my early learning from Abraham-Hicks and also conversations with Danielle about core desired feelings.

HOW DO YOU WANT TO FEEL?

Go back to your peak moments descriptions from the exercise you just completed and re-read them, either to yourself or to your partner, and notice what emotions were present in all of these experiences. A great way to do this systematically is to list every single emotion present in any of the descriptions. Then, each time an emotion shows up again, put a little tick mark next to it. If it shows up in just one of your peak moments, just write it down. Then if an emotion shows up in all three experiences, it will be written down on the list and have two tick marks next to it. Cool?

Once you've finished this, circle the emotions that showed up in all three peak moments. Put a star next to those that showed up in two out of three peak moments. These circled and starred emotions are how you want to feel.

There you have it. In a moment, we're going to take this handful of feeling words and couple it with your Peak Moments exercise to create a guide by which you can steer your financial life. But first, we have to explore one more mind-set.

OPENING YOURSELF TO HOW

Let me remind you—the only reason we want certain things is because we think they're going to make us feel a certain way. But sometimes we hold on so tightly to one idea of how we are going to get there that we miss other possible routes. And thus, we squelch the universe.

So why not skip directly to the good stuff? Why not go right for the feeling and surrender ourselves to the beautiful unfolding of the "how"?

For example, let's say Meredith desires to feel *free*. She's noticed in her Peak Moments exercise that *free* is an emotion that shows up in all three experiences. She notices that a common theme is that they all happened during a time in her life when she had more than enough money to support herself and she had no one to answer to. She was in her early 20s and she was traveling the world following her heart and her sense of adventure. Meredith's mouth is watering to feel that way again. So, she decides to work her butt off for a year to sock away enough money to go travel for a year and tap back into that state of freedom and adventure that was so intoxicating to her as a young woman.

It's all going great. Meredith is taking on more projects, working a lot of hours, and cranking away. Her savings account is growing and every day she looks at a collage of photos she created of places she can't wait to visit. She has a happy satisfaction, albeit a slightly burned-out version of it, knowing that every moment she puts in at the office is buying her time out in the world with nothing but a backpack and a dream.

Then, out of the blue, David shows up. David is quirkily handsome, has a twinkle in his eye, and works in the building next door. He's not at all Meredith's type as he's a bit soft around the middle, not particularly athletic, and more into home repair and gardening than scaling mountains and living under a tarp in the woods, as most of the men of her past have been. They first meet in line for their early-morning lattes at Starbucks. Though Meredith is initially hesitant to go out with him, after the fourth time he asks she finally says yes just to shut him up and make him go away.

Meredith is now four months away from her exit day. She has two-thirds of the money saved up to cut the strings with her corporate job and take off into the wild blue yonder for a year. It's so close that she can already taste the Vietnamese street food and smell the markets in Mumbai. She can feel the salty air of the Dead Sea on her skin and the sand of the Sahara between her toes. One dinner with David. That's all, just to get him off her back. She won't be thrown off her path. She wants freedom and the way to get it is to stay the course, work her butt off for four more months, and then head off.

She barely even looks in the mirror before heading out the door to meet David for dinner. Who cares how she looks? This isn't going to go anywhere anyway. Not if she has anything to do with it. One dinner. Thank you. Kiss on the cheek goodnight. And good-bye.

She walks into the restaurant with an exterior shell so thick it would take an ice pick to get through. Yet there's something in David's twinkly eyes that stirs a familiar sensation in her gut. It feels fluttery and expansive. It feels free. Her icy exterior begins to melt, dripping slowly onto the floor beneath her chair. Oh, shit. She feels simultaneously anxious, exhilarated, terrified, and irritated. By the end of dinner there's a pool of water at her feet that used to be her frigid shell. She sits in front of David, vulnerable, open, still slightly irritated, but most definitely intrigued.

He kisses her goodnight and the expansive feeling in her core gets bigger. She quickly ducks into her car, terrified to dive further into him for fear she might get lost in there. She's got a plan to stick with and this man could very well divert her from her well-laid path. She must never see him again, she agrees with herself driving home in the misty darkness. I want to feel free, she assures herself, and this man will trap me. Emotional ties bind us. Relationships are complicated. I want freedom and I'm so close to getting it. Just stay the course, Meredith, she whispers to herself. Stay the course and you'll be free in four months.

So Meredith ignores David's phone calls, the flowers he sends to her office, and his texts. She comes to work earlier and leaves later, hanging out in the lobby for a moment or two checking the street outside to ensure that she's not going to run into him. She starts bringing her coffee from home instead of going to Starbucks because she can't bear the potential of becoming unraveled when she sees David's quirky, sparkling eyes and that awkward but adorable smile.

The fourth month comes. Meredith has saved more than enough to make her departure. Her boss wishes her well with regret, she sublets her apartment, and packs up her bag. She chooses to ignore the heavy feeling she's harboring in her chest as she boards the plane to Bangkok, her jumping-off point for her year of freedom. She begins her travels, meets amazing people, relishes the beautiful sites, and enjoys dipping her toe into new cultures. But alone at night in the hostels she can't help but admit that she feels lonely. That expansive freedom she found across the world 15 years before is no longer here. If she were really honest with herself she'd notice that instead of free, she actually feels depressed. She's experiencing this adventure as though behind a plate-glass window, totally preoccupied for a longing she can't quite name.

As she sits on the beach on the Gold Coast of Australia one day all she can think about is the amount of spaciousness and possibility she felt when she was with David. His attempts at reaching out had stopped months ago, but an ember of potential still burns in her belly. "Meredith," she declares to herself, "we're going home!" And with that, she packs up and books a one-way ticket. Immediately her depressed fog starts to burn off and she catches a glimmer of the expansive enthusiasm she first felt when traveling long ago, when originally planning her trip, and when sitting over a white tablecloth with David.

She returns to her city and stays with a girlfriend who greets her at the door with a knowing look in her eye and says with faint sarcasm, "Back so soon?! I never would have guessed." Meredith waits a day or two and then phones David. The sheer act of dialing his number makes her feel so spacious that she can barely contain her giddiness. He's so thrilled to hear from her that he can only keep up his hurt, despondent act for a few moments. They agree to meet up that evening.

Meredith realizes that what she had flown across the world to feel, she feels right here with David. As they continue their relationship, they explore every nook and cranny of their own city and have crazy adventures in planting perennial beds in the backyard. They travel from time to time, but Meredith's itch to leave seems to have been scratched. Here, with this slightly roly-poly, adorable man, Meredith feels free. And she now knows that if she lost this expansive, free feeling, it would always come back, sourced from within, and sometimes presenting itself in the most unlikely of packages. She realizes that the freedom she'd felt in her early 20s exploring the world came from following her heart, not from traipsing around with a backpack. And here she is again, two blocks down from the apartment she'd felt trapped in for 15 years, following her heart, feeling free gardening and doing DIY projects with a man who thought camping was renting a cabin in the woods that came with a fully stocked refrigerator and turn-down service.

Ideally, we would spend our money on the things that are the most important to us, on the things that reflect our priorities, and on the things that bring us the most joy, satisfaction, and/or feelings of abundance, wealth, and freedom. But until we get clear on what we value, we can't get our financial life lined up with who we truly are. And until we let go of how we think it's supposed to look or how it will all turn out, we can't fully let the miracles our life has in store for us unfold.

NAVIGATING FREEDOM

Throughout this book, we've been working our way to a greater sense of freedom. Freedom is choice. Freedom doesn't necessarily mean opting to do crazy, wild things or living a life vastly outside the box. But it's the option to do so should you choose. One time my family was visiting my aunt and uncle and their three boys. My sister and I were fascinated by "the guys" as we called them because we grew up in the land of pink and fairies and they grew up in the land of sports, slingshots, and trying to take one another out on at least an hourly basis. My sister and I wanted to spend the afternoon with them but our dad told us no. He was afraid that if we stayed with them we would watch TV all afternoon (worse fates could have befallen us, but he was quite concerned about our media intake). My sister was totally pissed and in her very proper and far-beyond-her-years way, she replied, "It is not that I would choose to watch television, Dad. It's that I would like to have the choice."

Those words from 11-year-old Ann pretty much sum it up. It's not always that we'll choose what's in front of us, it's that we would like to have the freedom to do so if we felt compelled.

The thing about freedom, though, is that it can be overwhelming, and at times debilitating. As humans we actually thrive on structure. The seasons in most places in the world define what we put on in the morning and what activities we can do each day and whether they're inside or outside. Our upbringing and desire to fit in give us a framework from which to make choices. And then there's the whole bit about other people's expectations of us, a set of parameters that, I would argue, informs the choices of way too many human beings. (And, as I posited at the beginning of this chapter, a set of parameters that caused and continues to cause a worldwide economic crisis.)

How do we enjoy true freedom of choice while still having some sort of framework to use when making choices so that we're not lost at sea like a little rowboat without any oars, rudder, or mooring? I'm so glad you asked. Enter the "Touchstones of Freedom," which was inspired by Danielle LaPorte's core desired feelings concept that I mentioned before.

TOUCHSTONES OF FREEDOM

The Merriam-Webster dictionary defines *touchstone* as "a fundamental or quintessential part or feature." Basically, this means that a touchstone is something that helps define an event or a person.

This is important for you because now is the time when we're going to pull together the touchstones of your life—what feelings and values define the truest version of you. Living in accordance with these will lead to you living a life of freedom, which is why I refer to these as Touchstones of Freedom.

So here's how you do it. In your Money Love Journal, write down the emotions that you identified in the How Do You Want to Feel? exercise, and then write down your values from the What Do You Value? exercise.

After you've identified these guiding principles, go to www.moneyalovestory.com/touchstones and download the Touchstones of Freedom PDF. Print it, write your desired feelings and your values on the card, cut it out, get it laminated, and stick it in your wallet. Even better, print out several, write them out, decorate them however you wish, laminate them, and place them around your home and office for regular reminders of who you are and what makes you tick.

These Touchstones of Freedom can serve as your guide for every financial decision you make from here until eternity. Any time you're not sure whether to say yes or no to a spending choice, an investment, an opportunity, a collaboration, a new project, a trip, or even an invitation, pull out your Touchstones. What's freeing about this guide is that you never have to be lost again, floating in a sea of choices without any structure. When faced with a choice, pull out your card and read through the way you want to feel and your values. Ask yourself, will saying yes to this move me toward the way I want to feel and my values or will it move me away from these essential parts of my true self? This may require a bit of future projection on your part, because we never know 100 percent where a decision is taking us, but listen to your body. Your body will either feel contracted or expanded. Go for expanded. Again, your body never lies. Read your Touchstones, listen to your body, and I guarantee you'll make the financial decision that's best for you in that moment.

LINE IT UP

Let's dive in a little further to the concept of spending in line with your values. Sadly, much of the time, our spending habits don't do this. We invest in a mutual fund that our financial advisor thinks is a good idea or we buy a certificate of deposit because our dad thinks it's a safe, secure choice. We spend more than feels good on a dress to look like a million bucks at our high school reunion because we want to "look good" even though signing the credit card slip made our stomach turn. We buy a house that's bigger than we need, or even really want, because of our mother-in-law's judgment of our cozy bungalow. To live a life that feels truly free we must get our spending aligned with our values.

So it's time to get out a magnifying glass and examine our spending choices in the context of our motivation and what purpose we were aiming to serve with each choice. Let's see if your spending choices are in alignment with your Touchstones of Freedom. And if not, we'll get you turned in the right direction so that your spending choices coincide with your desired feelings and values. Then it'll be smooth sailing.

SPENDING MOTIVATION

Part 1: Out-of-Line Buys

We've already done the first piece of work in our efforts to spend in line with our values. Remember the exercise we did in Chapter 4 about finding potential financial energy leaks? Open your Money Love Journal to your list of energy leaks (though if it's been a while since you did this exercise, you may want to do it again with more recent bills and credit-card statements).

Transfer the list of transactions that felt bad (along with the date, the amount, and what was purchased) on to a new page in your Money Love Journal titled Spending Motivation.

Now, look at what you listed and go a little deeper. Were there any other people involved in this spending decision, either directly or indirectly? Was it really your husband's desire to make this purchase and you went along with it even though it didn't feel good to you? Did you make this purchase because you didn't feel like dealing with the flak you'd receive from your mother for not having the perfect patio furniture? Now, write down what the circumstances were around the transaction. Be as detailed as you'd like here. You may find that this exercise opens up a can of worms and suddenly you're doing a freewrite about feeling controlled by your mother. That's really good! Let it all out. You have to feel it to heal it. In order for our financial lives to get lined up with how we want to feel and what we value, we first have to become aware of and release the influences that have had a hold on our financial decisions up until this point in our lives.

Part 2: In-Line Buys

Now that you've identified purchases that made you feel bad, we're going to flip things around and look at it from the positive side. Grab your financial statements, and look at the expenses that don't have a dot by them. Transfer those into your Money Love Journal along with the date, what the transaction was for, and any details about the circumstance. Were you buying party supplies for a gathering of people you love in your home? Were you putting a deposit on your first apartment of your own? How did you feel when you made these spending choices?

Look back over the list you just made of transactions that felt good or expansive when you made them and take out your Touchstones of Freedom. Next to each transaction, write down the emotion and/or value that it represents from your lists of desired feelings and values. Notice how good it feels to spend money in a way that actually represents what you value. This is what money was made for. That's why it feels good when we spend in this way.

Keep this exercise in mind as you make future spending decisions. When you go to make a payment, check in with how your body feels. Get your Touchstones of Freedom out and see if this decision lines up. If it doesn't, is there a way that you could make a different choice? There are very few circumstances when you're totally trapped into making a decision that doesn't feel good. Start to think expansively and as the empowered financial steward you are. This is your money. You get to choose. If your decision feels good and is in alignment with your Touchstones of Freedom, congratulations! You're exercising your human right of free will and conscious choice. Nice work.

Every time you sit down with your money, meet with a member of your financial team, or have a conversation about money with your spouse or family, keep your Touchstones of Freedom either with you physically or at least present in your mind. Make long-term financial plans according to your Touchstones instead of according to the statistics or equations that your financial planner might give you. You get to organize your financial life around what does it for you. You are a beautifully unique individual and your financial plan doesn't have to be like anyone else's. If you base it on how you want to feel and your values, you can't go wrong. This is the only way that money buys us happiness: when we line it up with who we truly are.

Chapter 8

TRUE FINANCIAL FREEDOM

At this point in our journey together you've begun to unravel some of your money "stuff" and you're getting clarity on where your money is going, what you value, and how you can add more value to the world. Your financial life is lining up more with the truth of who you are.

For some of you this will be as far as you go. You may have gotten to the point where you feel good in your finances. You feel free from the worry about needing to pay the rent or buy groceries—or even taking that trip you've been wanting to take. However, I would argue that even though you've reached this point, there's still farther you can go—if you choose to do so.

If you want to create a life of true financial freedom, you not only need to consider how much you're spending and how much you make, you also need to consider the source of your income. As you read through this chapter, what I lay out may be too scary to think about right now. Or you may think that what I'm proposing is not for you. Or this may speak to your soul and inspire you to think about your finances in an even more expansive way. Whatever rings true is the right way to go. Just remember, you are wonderful as you are, and if you decide that this step is right for you—even if it's not right now—I know that you can do it.

DIFFERENT TYPES OF DOLLARS

Just like all calories are not equal, not every dollar of earned income is equal. Eating 1,000 calories of donuts will have a different effect on your body and the way you feel than eating 1,000 calories of spinach. Consider earning $1,000 working at a job that's not in alignment with your values. It has a different quality from earning $1,000 by doing something that you're deeply passionate about.

"Now wait," you say. "There's a lot of room in between doing something you hate and doing something you love." And of course I agree. So let's start to look at some distinctions. Let's look at three scenarios: 1) you work for a tyrant, doing a job you hate that doesn't use your talents; 2) you work for a wonderful boss doing a job that pays you well and that you enjoy; and 3) you create a digital download based on your work that will continue to bring in money without you doing more to the product.

These scenarios address two important things to consider when evaluating income sources: alignment with who you are, and linear vs. leveraged income. It is my sincere wish for you that you do work that you love and that feels aligned with the truth of who you are. If this were the only bedrock of what I believe is true financial freedom, scenarios 2 and 3 would be equally beneficial.

That said, the difference between linear and leveraged income gives you the option of creating leverage in your life that you would not otherwise have access to.

Therefore, let's get straight on these two different kinds of income now. Money made trading hours for dollars, or linear income, comes from getting paid a certain amount of money for an amount of time worked or a specific service provided. This is basically the income you get for working at a company or for yourself. Leveraged income is income that is not 100 percent proportional to the time worked or the service provided. For example, leveraged income can come from the repeat sale of a product you created once, from repeat sales commissions, from rental income, from investments, and from business systems. It's considered leveraged because it gives you more leverage on your time and energy since you get paid more than once for your investment of your time and skills.

There are many paths to making money that don't include trading hours for dollars. Having several streams of income from a variety of leveraged sources gives you utmost access to financial freedom. But for now, since you may be new to the concept of leveraged income in the first place, let's just look at the theory behind this type of income. And if you're inspired after you read this, check out the Appendix, which outlines a number of different ways you can create this type of income.

THE CASHFLOW QUADRANT

When I read Robert Kiyosaki's book *Rich Dad, Poor Dad* at the end of high school, the tectonic plates shifted under my feet and I was a changed human being. Never again would I think about earning money in the same way. Kiyosaki planted a seed of freedom in me that has grown into some serious foliage over the years.

There were two concepts in the book that particularly rocked my world. One was the financial freedom equation that states that we are financially free when our leveraged income is greater than our living expenses. My quest for financial freedom centered on making this equation true in my own life.

The second concept is the Cashflow Quadrant. To dive really deeply into this stuff I recommend getting *Rich Dad, Poor Dad* and studying this material. For our purposes I'll give you an overview to whet your appetite. The Cashflow Quadrant diagram is below:

CASHFLOW QUADRANT is reproduced with permission of CASHFLOW Technologies, Inc. Copyright ©2011 by Robert T. Kiyosaki, *Rich Dad's CASHFLOW Quadrant: Rich Dad's Guide to Financial Freedom,* Plata Publishing, LLC.

The *E* stands for Employee, the *S* for Self-Employed, the *B* for Business Owner, and the *I* for Investor. In the ultimate version of financial freedom, the goal is to move from the left side of the diagram, where *E* and *S* live, to the right side, where *B* and *I* live. As an employee or a self-employed person, you have very little leverage. You are only paid for your own efforts, not the efforts of anyone else or any other system. And you have nothing in place to get paid multiple times on a single effort, like you would if you wrote a book or created a digital product.

Those on the *E* and *S* side are also more highly taxed than those on the *B* and *I* side because they have fewer opportunities to decrease their tax burden. Of all the wealth in the world, 5 percent is earned on the left side of the diagram, and 95 percent is earned on the right side. Interestingly, though, 95 percent of people are on the left side of the diagram, whereas 5 percent are on the right side.

On the *B* and *I* side, your money works hard for you instead of you working hard for your money. Business Owners own systems that work for them whether they show up or not. An example would be Warren Buffett who owns, among other things, a company called The Pampered Chef. I guarantee you that Buffet does not need to show up at the office every day in order for this high-quality cookware to be sold and for revenue to be generated. There's a system in place that's not dependent upon his time or effort anymore. Someone who is in the *I* quadrant has investments that are growing their money. They might invest in paper assets like stocks and bonds, in real estate, or in businesses. Generally speaking, if you're looking to create true financial freedom, you'll want to take the money generated from your B-quadrant business and invest it.

Don't worry, the transition from left to right—*E* and *S* to *B* and *I*—can mature quite a lot while you're still on the left. You don't have to make a transition overnight. You also don't have to make the transition completely. It's perfectly wonderful to earn some of your money from the left side and some of it from the right side. However, it's important to really understand the differences between the different quadrants, and their respective advantages and disadvantages.

One of the most common things I see is that people who are employees want freedom so they start their own business and become self-employed. There's absolutely nothing inherently wrong with starting your own business or being self-employed, but it's certainly not a tried-and-true path to freedom. Most self-employed people leave a job in order to call the shots, make their own hours, and not have to answer to anyone else. But what they end up doing is in essence just being owned by their job because if they don't show up, nothing happens and no revenue is generated. They are left holding the bag and more often than not this leads to tremendous stress, 80-hour work weeks, and burnout.

Let's take Nancy as an example. Nancy is a highly skilled massage therapist in Miami. She works for one of the big hotels on South Beach doing in-room and spa massages. She likes the fact that she has benefits and that she gets paid time off, but she hates that someone else is in charge of when she works, who her clients are, and what she can charge.

Nancy, being the freedom-seeking kind of girl that she is, decides to open her own massage therapy practice.

She's pretty well connected in Miami and knows that between her high-end clientele where she'll make house calls and then her other clients who'll come see her at her rented office space, she'll be able to fill up her schedule without a problem.

And she's right. Within a month of hanging up her shingle, Nancy's Healing Hands Massage is booming. She's booked a month out with a waiting list, sees clients in the office three days a week, and then makes house calls three days a week. She's doing up to six massages a day and raking in great money. She's exhausted each night when she comes home, but it's the sweet satisfied sort of exhausted that comes from doing great work, reaping the benefits of your own efforts, and helping people.

Six months after starting her business Nancy breaks her arm playing beach volleyball after a particularly dramatic spike. The doctor tells her she can't move her arm, let alone give a massage, for three months. What? Nancy freaks out because she has no income coming in other than what she can earn when she shows up to give a massage. She has just slightly over a thousand dollars in savings and no one to ask for financial help. Suddenly, she doesn't feel so free.

Nancy is the classic example of an S-quadrant person. She's a go-getter, she's dynamic, and she wants freedom. She's a natural-born leader and she's always had the belief that if you want something done right you should do it yourself. Which, of course, is the kiss of death for the self-employed. Their income is completely dependent upon them showing up and doing everything, so if for some reason they can't show up, no money is made.

Some people like Nancy decide that they don't want everything to be 100 percent dependent on them in terms of income generation so they hire employees. Nancy could hire five great massage therapists in Miami, for example, and take a cut from every massage they give. But now she's added the headache of employees to the picture and worrying about how her brand is represented by people she has no control over. This is the price that many of us believe we must pay for freedom.

In order to be truly free, though, we must get over needing to do everything ourselves. We must get over thinking that we've failed somehow if we ask for help, and we must get over needing to control everything. If you want to become wealthy, hire people who are smarter and more talented, or who have better skills than you do. Get people on your team whom you look up to.

Let's say that Nancy has an enterprising friend named Jason. He's done very well in the stock market, and they met living the high life on South Beach one night. Jason hears about Nancy's predicament and decides that there's a great opportunity here for both of them. She needs money and he needs a new project. He's always been passionate about health and Nancy seems to have become the most sought-after massage therapist in all of Miami. She has a specific technique to relieve upper back and shoulder tension that you can't find anywhere else.

Nancy has always kept this technique a closely guarded secret because it's been the key to keeping her clients coming back. But Jason helps her see it another way. He paints a picture of true freedom for her if she's willing to give up control. If she were to teach a team of other massage therapists this technique and license them to use it under her brand name, she could make great, recurring income from her "invention." So, after some convincing and some time on Nancy's part having to come to terms with her control issues, Jason invests a chunk of money and they go to work.

Nancy trains her first class of massage therapists in her shoulder and neck tension release technique, which she has now trademarked and branded. Every massage therapist whom she trains gets to use the technique and run their own business, but they pay her each year to use her brand because the technique has become so popular. This way she doesn't have to deal with employing any other massage therapists—they're required to come to continuing education with her and other master trainers at her company if they want to continue to use the brand to build their clientele, and she gets a big paycheck every time one of her therapists renews their licensing agreement. She's also ensured that she's well protected by the law in terms of intellectual property.

Nancy and Jason then start investing their earnings from this new B-quadrant business into various real estate and business deals in Miami. Some of them do great, and a few tank, but overall their bottom line remains strong because of their cash cow business. They are both totally financially free *and* they get to do work that's in their zone of genius, which they've clarified along the way. Plus they've set up a system through which other massage therapists can get better at what they do and build lucrative practices for themselves. They even have a referral program so that when a massage therapist refers another massage therapist to the training to get licensed, they earn a percentage of the licensing fee each year so they can have some residual income, too. Everybody wins!

Nancy's story is just one example of how an employee moves to the *S* quadrant and then graduates to living the life of freedom on the *B* and *I* quadrants.

THE MYTH OF INDISPENSABILITY

We've all been taught that the way to get ahead in life is to work really hard for everything and prove ourselves. We've also been taught to become totally indispensable in order to ensure job security and success. Become the best, most specialized, highly skilled widget maker and you'll always have a place to work and a steady paycheck. Build a business around your unique skills, gifts, and talents and make sure that you're the only one who can do what you do. That way you'll never be replaced or eclipsed by someone else.

Here's the problem with this mentality: if you're indispensable, you're stuck. If you're the very best at what you do and no one else can possibly do it the way you do, that means you have to show up to do it. In order for any production to happen and for revenue to be generated, you have to be there.

If you're going for job security, perhaps becoming indispensable is the way to do it. But if you're going for true financial freedom, it's time to let yourself be dispensable. You can't go for job security and freedom simultaneously. The two are sort of mutually exclusive and as goals, they stem from two entirely different mind-sets.

And the truth is, job security is a myth anyway. There are so many players and external factors inherent in all business that there is no assurance that things will remain the same—especially in this day and age. Putting your future and financial life completely in the hands of your boss or your boss's boss or some corporation isn't necessarily the smartest thing you can do in your quest for freedom.

Therefore, if you're going for freedom you have to become dispensable in some kind of B-quadrant business. This concept is challenging to grasp, especially for the ego. "You mean, I have to make it so that I'm not necessary in order for the system to work and so that it doesn't matter if I'm there or not?" you may say. And my answer is a resounding YES! If you want to be truly financially free, that is.

When you're considering your path to financial freedom, make sure to consider all the different facets of your goal. I often hear people say that they want to be famous because famous people are rich and free. But I say, if you want to be famous and feel important, that's something entirely different. I suggest you dig a little deeper into what's behind your desire for fame. If you have a deep need to be seen, that's great. You don't have to be famous to be seen. You can try out for a theater production or musical group and find out how it feels to be seen while on stage. Begin to love and acknowledge yourself more. Deepen your personal relationships so you can feel more seen there. Then you can create a life that doesn't require fame but that still helps you fulfill that need to be seen—and you can create a life that doesn't require that you show up all the time in order for money to be made.

If you want to be famous to live the crazy celebrity life, then yes, go for it, but don't assume that being famous is synonymous with being rich or having financial freedom. That combination is not a foregone conclusion. Here's a little of my personal experience with these phenomena: When I was in middle school my mom's book *Women's Bodies, Women's Wisdom* started getting a lot of attention. From the time the book was published when I was 11 to now she's been on Oprah ten times, has made *The New York Times* bestseller list more than once, and has spoken to many a packed auditorium.

People would ask me all the time, "What's it like to have a rich and famous mother?" It was an inherently difficult question to answer, given that I've only ever had one mother and I have nothing to compare it to. I still get ruffled to this day when people ask me that. What's fascinating about it for the purposes of our conversation, though, is that people automatically equate being famous with being rich. There's an assumption that when you become well-known you suddenly have a whole bunch of money and are financially free.

I'm so glad I had the experience of growing up with a well-known mom who's also incredibly down to earth because it taught me a lot about priorities. I've also spent quite a bit of time with well-known actors, musicians, and other folks in high-profile positions. And I'm here to report that being well-known doesn't necessarily make you rich, and it certainly doesn't make you smart with money. There are hundreds of stories of people making a lot of money and then not managing it well so that just a few years later they have nothing.

Willie Nelson is a great example. He's a household name and many might assume that he's rich, as well. He may be doing okay now, but he had to file bankruptcy in 1990 because he owed $16.7 million in back taxes to the IRS. To his credit, he got creative and released an album called *The IRS Tapes: Who'll Buy My Memories?*, which he sold to pay back what he owed. But my point remains: being famous doesn't necessarily mean you'll make a lot of money. Plus, if you do make a lot of money, that in and of itself doesn't necessarily build wealth because it's what you do with the money that really matters.

The other thing being well-known doesn't guarantee is being happy or feeling loved. In the film *J. Edgar* starring Leonardo DiCaprio, there's a line that really stuck with me. A woman J. Edgar is spending some time with says to him, "All the admiration in the world can't fill the spot where love goes." So soberingly true.

If you want to go out in the world and make a huge difference, some notoriety may come along with it, and there's nothing wrong with that. But when it comes to your financial life and setting yourself up for true freedom, my recommendation is to make it so that your income, or the bulk of it, is not dependent upon you showing up and producing, no matter how well-known or impactful you become.

There are some places where becoming dispensable makes no sense. With your friends and family, obviously you want to be the best, most unique version of yourself and show up fully. When it comes to doing your creative work, the work that you were born to do, the things that are in your zone of genius, you of course want to let your light shine and be the best, most extraordinary *you* that you can be. But when it comes to leverage, you can't be indispensable and financially free at the same time.

GETTIN' NITTY-GRITTY WITH IT

This is a good time for a reminder of what it means to be truly financially free. My definition is twofold. The first part is purely mathematical: you are financially free when your passive or residual (leveraged) income is greater than your living expenses. Very simple and clear. And for many people the hardest part of this equation is not earning enough leveraged income, but instead getting clear and honest about their living expenses (revisit Chapter 5 if you need some review on this).

The second part of my personal definition of financial freedom is less tangible, but no doubt equally important. This part says that you're financially free to the degree that money trips you up far less often, that you have a loving relationship with your money, and that you truly value yourself and your contribution in the world. This is financial freedom on the emotional and spiritual side of things. Just like enlightenment, achieving this level of freedom is a practice and may not be 100 percent achieved in this lifetime. But little by little we can value ourselves a little bit more each day, we can show up more fully in life to provide value, and we can heal our relationship with money baby step by baby step, well into our 90s or beyond.

For now we're going to dive into different ways to create leveraged income: residual, passive, or recurring. First, I'll define those three terms.

- **Residual income:** income that comes in over and over again for work you did one time (e.g. royalties on books, earnings from acting in a commercial and getting paid each time it airs, or repeat commissions income from one initial sale of a consumable like vitamins, skin care, or a food product)

- **Passive income:** income that comes in from investments—it feels passive because you're not showing up to a certain place at a certain time to earn it (e.g. rental income on a property you own or dividends on stocks)

- **Recurring income:** similar to residual income, in that it comes from work you do once and then get paid over and over again for—the difference is that these payments come on a set timeline

Anyone who tells you that creating residual, passive, or recurring income doesn't require work is misinformed. All of these types of income require strategy, skill, time, energy, and at times, capital, to put in place. These types of income pay you multiple times on the original work that you put in. If you have a job or are self-employed, on the other hand, you put in the same work and energy but you only get paid once for it. You see the difference? Both require energy and work, but the first one is much smarter and the second one is simply harder. If you're going to work anyway, why not get paid on it multiple times?

Since I read *Rich Dad, Poor Dad* I've been rewired to think in terms of recurring income. Coaching and offering workshops is a linear income model and making my money that way fundamentally goes against my entire financial philosophy (though there's nothing wrong with it for other people). That's why I closed my feng shui consultation business, even though it was thriving and I was making great money. I couldn't stand that the hours I spent working with my clients were traded for dollars and that there was no recurring income built into the business model. Find a client, work for a few hours, get paid. Repeat. Over and over again. I just couldn't do it anymore.

I launched my Mentoring Program in February 2012. I'd built a significant online following, and I realized there was no clear way for people to work with me when they came to my site. I knew that I could start to coach people on financial freedom or offer workshops, but that's a linear income model: work once, get paid once. When I launched the program, I was overwhelmed by the positive response. I had more than 50 applicants for 12 spots in the first weeks of the launch, and I was thrilled. What the applicants were applying for was a spot in my network marketing business with USANA where they would get to work with my team, The Freedom Family, and also get to work one-on-one with me. I took 11 years of business experience and training that I gained while creating financial freedom for myself and a six-figure business and put it into the content for this Mentoring Program. And the only thing people had to do to join was start a business with USANA (which was a very small investment of less than $1,000).

What was fascinating about talking to all of the applicants is how many of them just wanted to pay me for my time but didn't want to start a business. They would have paid me upward of $4,000 just to work with me one-on-one, but they couldn't see the value in starting their own residual income business for less than $1,000 as a ticket to work with me. People are fascinating. They really are. Granted, a network marketing business isn't for everyone, but here's what I learned from the experience: many people would rather throw money in the direction of their desires than take action to move toward them.

I know I could coach and work with people one-on-one or in groups. I know I could make a lot of money that way, and perhaps I will in the future—who knows? But I believe so strongly in creating recurring income streams in my life that I don't want to spend any of my precious time investing in streams of income where I can only get paid once for the effort I put in. Some people think I'm nuts and I've had to turn away a lot of potential clients and have had some criticism from peers. But I value freedom down to my core and my kind of freedom is created through recurring income. I can't be off coaching people one-on-one making linear income in one area of my life and then standing on stage talking about the importance of freedom and residual income. It makes no sense. So that's why, at least right now, the only way you can work with me one-on-one is to join my USANA business. That way we both earn residual income together with a proven business model in an industry that works with a product line that I adore and is the best thing you can get for your health. It's a total win-win. And I would feel hypocritical offering anything else at this point.

This choice is because of how integral financial freedom and leverage are to my mission and how I want to be of service to others. If you're a person who's interested in financial freedom but also likes to engage in forms of income generation that are linear, please remember that these things are not by any means mutually exclusive, and you can trust your own instincts about what is the right mix and direction for you, your gifts and talents, and your goals. In order to help you determine this, let's look at some of the options for creating leveraged income.

YOUR NEXT STEP TO TRUE FINANCIAL FREEDOM

As we've already discussed, plans for the big changes in life need to be put together as a series of finite action steps so you don't get overwhelmed and discouraged. Our goal right now is simply to brainstorm possible ways for you to move into true financial freedom.

Grab your Money Love Journal, and start writing options for you to begin to create something that will give you leveraged income. For inspiration, flip to the Appendix and read the pros and cons of some of the different ways to do this. But don't be constrained by them! Use your imagination. Only you will know what you might want.

Once you've brainstormed some ideas, go back and see if you can identify which one would be best for you. Listen to your body and your intuition. Don't let the bigness of what you've imagined scare you away. Just write down one concrete action step that you can do in order to move in the direction of this goal. For example, if you want to start a network marketing business and you have a friend who invited you to a presentation a couple of months ago that you couldn't attend, your next finite action step could be to "e-mail Susan and ask her if she'd go to coffee with me next Tuesday to hear a presentation about her business."

Now, put that action step in your calendar on a specific date at a specific time. The act of identifying your next action step and putting it into your calendar will make you feel infinitely less overwhelmed.

If financial freedom is your ultimate goal, you have to stop thinking that the only way to create it is to work more hours, ask for a raise, go back to school for an advanced degree, or charge higher rates. Instead, you must start considering ways of making money that free up your time, the ultimate commodity. There is no one right way for everyone, so pick a means of creating leveraged income that resonates with you and then start taking the baby steps necessary to make it grow.

Conclusion

BUT SERIOUSLY, WHAT'S THE POINT?

It's great to get your own money house cleaned up, as well as to make more than enough money to have the lifestyle you dream of. But then what? What really is the point of all the work we've been doing anyway?

We've all heard someone say it: "You can't take it with you." That's why my philosophy isn't about accumulation. It's about freedom. My passion for creating financial freedom comes from a deep knowing that I want to make the world a better place while I'm here. And my reason for teaching what I've learned is that I know that each of us is here for a reason. We can't show up to our purpose as fully if we're constantly worried about finances. If we're stressed-out about paying the rent and putting food on the table it puts a damper on our creative energy. Financial stress takes up bandwidth, period, and makes it much harder to hear your soul's calling.

And from my perspective, the point of getting yourself freed up financially is really so that you can show up to your purpose on the planet and, by doing so, make a meaningful contribution. One of my favorite quotes is by Frederick Buechner, who says, "The place God calls you to is the place where your deep gladness and the world's deep hunger meet." Where is that place you're called to? Now that the static of financial stress has died down, it's a good time to revisit your passion. I don't care if you're called to be an amazing, present mother, take ballroom dance classes all day, or fund an orphanage in Uganda. Whatever it may be, move toward the place of your deepest gladness because by the sheer act of feeling fulfilled and following your heart, you are serving the planet.

I already mentioned that studies have shown that people tend to take action more to avoid pain than they do to move toward pleasure. Chances are pretty good that some of the previous chapters helped you tell the truth about your financial situation and perhaps that was painful. I know when I started to get really honest with myself about my money it was painful. But it wasn't as painful as staying stuck in financial unconsciousness with a nagging feeling that I was living without integrity. There was something tremendously freeing about starting to tell the truth and look at my money in a new way. And my financial reality began to shift dramatically very soon after I started looking at it with consciousness, clarity, and love. I started to make more money, I got my debt paid off, I achieved true financial freedom, and I began to add more value to the world by getting my authentic voice out there through writing, speaking, and mentoring.

Chances are pretty good that right now you're in touch with the pain of financial upheaval or unconsciousness. And at this point you've put some systems in place to move away from that pain and toward the pleasure of financial consciousness and freedom. You may not be there yet, but you're on your way, which feels great. The difference between standing still and moving forward, even if it's one baby step at a time, is significant and shouldn't be overlooked.

Now is a good time to congratulate yourself for making it this far on your money love journey. A lot of people bail along the way because they get too scared or they let their resistance get the better of them. So take a moment to celebrate a job well done. What we focus our attention on grows. The more you practice celebrating your successes, no matter how small, the more you'll have to celebrate.

Now is also a good time to revisit the Money Love Quiz at the front of this book. Retake the quiz and see how your score has improved. Keep coming back to that quiz in the months and years to follow and see how you are tangibly falling more deeply in love with your money, yourself, and your life.

I would never be so bold as to suggest that I know the reason why we're here on earth, as that remains one of life's most eternal and unanswerable questions. But I'm pretty sure we weren't put here to struggle and to work in jobs we hate. I know that there aren't any two people who are exactly alike and there has to be a reason for that. You are totally unique. You are unlike any other. You have gifts to share with the world that no one else can share. And if you go through your life miserable, broke, and feeling trapped, the world will never experience your gifts.

So, if you need yet another reason to get your finances in order and set yourself free, do it because you owe your full-throttle brilliance to the planet.

I began my journey of creating financial freedom because I want to be a really present mama someday. I want to be able to focus on my family and be home with my little nuggets while they're young. I want to spend a lot of time hanging out at the beach, making sand castles and reading stories with them, making sure they know they're precious. I can't think of a more worthy endeavor than being present with little ones. It's an investment in a brighter future for the planet, and it will probably save thousands in therapy bills for them later on.

But maybe that's not your thing. Maybe you're a contortionist and you long to inspire large audiences with your feats of human talent. Or maybe you excel in the land of itemization and systemization and your personal path to world peace is through organization. Maybe you're exhausted and burned-out and thinking of some sort of noble cause right now is giving you a headache. You can't see beyond sitting by a pool somewhere warm drinking frothy beverages with mini umbrellas in them. That's cool, too. Following your bliss to that pool and hanging out there until you finally feel rested is definitely the way to go. Fill your energetic cup full first, even if it's bigger than that pool you're lounging beside. Eventually something in you will stir when you're finally filled and your own cup begins to overflow. And you'll want to direct that overflow somewhere meaningful that gives value in the world. Trust the process.

Whatever you're doing or wherever you are in your financial journey, now is the time to start thinking and acting as though you can do anything you want and as though you can have a significant impact on the world, because you can.

But Rome was not built in a day, my dear, and neither is financial freedom—it took me a good ten years, walking a very winding, indirect path, and I'm still on that journey. Some people will get there faster than me. Some slower. Some will dip their toe into financial freedom and freak out from the sheer possibility and expansiveness of it all and retreat. Perhaps someday they will come on back to taste that sweet nectar again and again. It doesn't matter how fast or slow you get there, it simply matters that you're moving and that you're choosing to become more and more financially conscious every day. Every step is a step forward. Once you begin, no matter what outside appearances might indicate, there's no such thing as a step backward. You're making progress, I promise.

WARTS AND ALL

Before I send you off on your own, I want to reinforce something I've mentioned throughout the book. We've been taught to believe that we'll be happy when we have flat abs, the perfect boyfriend, a beautiful home, a gurgling baby, our dream job, a six-figure business, and enough passive income to cover our living expenses. To me, this is a trap. No matter what you do, there will always be something you're working on. Life isn't about perfection. Life is about living.

Being happy is not about having your finances squared away or having certain things in your life. It would be insane and actually sadistic to suggest that you had to wait to be fulfilled until you get everything "fixed." When I was struggling with debt and the willingness to get financially conscious a loving but misguided friend told me, "You'll probably meet your man when you get all of your money stuff taken care of." Ugh. So we have to be perfect in order to find love? You mean I have to have a clean house, an organized sock drawer, a morning meditation practice, toned thighs, good credit, and a high salary to deserve and attract love from myself or anyone else? Well that just sucks.

Luckily, it's not true. I met a great man while I was still in debt. And I think it's not a coincidence that within six months of falling in love with him I had paid off all of my debt and within a year my income had more than doubled. I had been operating under the erroneous belief that I had to get myself completely perfect before I could be loved. But what I've come to know is that to be happy, you have to love yourself first, warts and all. You have to follow your own bliss.

Yes, becoming financially free is a great thing, but it's also not to be pursued in an obsessive way or in any way that compromises your happiness in the present moment. There's a great Thich Nhat Hanh quote that says, "There is no way to peace—peace is the way." Do what it takes to organize your life around that. Revisit your Touchstones of Freedom. Rock your own world even if you don't have the perfect body, job, man, woman, child, house, family, business, or tons of money in the bank. Every area of our life is connected, so the more you give yourself permission to be happy and enjoy any area of your life, the more this attitude and approach will rub off on other areas.

I'll never forget the moment I sat at my mom's kitchen table and paid off the last of my credit card debt. I was alone. It was July. I pressed "Submit" on the American Express website and it was done. Seven years of angst and stress zeroed out. I had done affirmations about having zero balances on my credit cards. I had printed off statements and whited out the balance and put in zeroes and stuck them on my vision board. And then it came true. I was finally debt-free.

I felt a surge of energy in my body in that moment, but mostly it was a quiet, serene satisfaction that I felt. I savored the initial feeling of paying it off for a while, wanting to make sure I remembered the moment and took it in fully. I told my mom and my man. They were thrilled for me. We went out to dinner to celebrate.

And then I went on with my life. Can I say that I'm happier as a result of being debt-free and financially free? Yeah, I would say that I am. But not because of the money. I'm happier now because I'm living in alignment with my values of freedom and service. I'm able to do more in the world, turn up the volume on my voice, add more value, and be more present because I'm not worried about my debt and how I'm going to pay it off. The rug burn in my brain caused by beating myself up about going unconscious around money has almost entirely healed. I'm now able to make decisions more from a place of how I want to feel and how I can be in service to my goals and the divine instead of from a place of wondering whether or not I'm going to be able to meet my credit card payment this month.

But I didn't wait until my credit card balances were zero or until I was making six figures to allow bliss into my life. I didn't wait to listen to my heart or to follow my passion. I didn't wait to do good work in the world or speak my truth or fall in love. And I don't recommend you wait either.

NOW WHAT?

It's such a freaking miracle that there is even life in this universe, let alone that we exist as sentient, relatively conscious human beings. That our hearts beat, that our eyelashes flutter, and that our minds open is pure magic. No matter how much scientists can explain about the cell and reproduction and how life works and continues to propagate, no one can really explain how we got here . . . or why. In my mind, there's no other way to look at it than to fill in the gaps between science and mystery with the divine.

Call it believing in something bigger than yourself, call it source, call it God, call it Goddess, call it the universe, call it that which you can't fully understand or articulate but that you know is there anyway. Call it what keeps you warm at night and keeps a spark of awe in your life. Call it magic. Call it a miracle. Whatever you choose to call it, there is something bigger than us at work and to me that explains the fact that we are all here, bumbling around this green-and-blue planet, each of us completely and totally unique.

You are a miracle. You are a freaking beautiful miracle. You are not an accident. You have something of tremendous value to offer the world, the universe, eternity. And allowing your life to be taken up by financial struggle and strife is playing smaller than you're capable of. Spending more than you make, living paycheck to paycheck, and going deeper into debt are not in service of you shining and lighting up the world.

I hope by this point in your reading you have a new perspective. I hope that you see a way out of financial stress and that you're well on the path to freedom. And I hope that you understand that financial freedom is about way more than just being able to pay your bills on time or making six figures. It's about way more than going out to nice dinners and taking vacations. (Though it's not *not* about those things either.) It's about fully embodying your gifts in this lifetime. It's about speaking the unique truth that only you are capable of articulating in the precise way that you do. It's about sharing your once-in-an-eternity version of brilliance with the world. And it's about doing it with an open-hearted relaxation and sense of enoughness, both of which can often be well facilitated by the state of being financially nourished.

Your financial well-being is directly linked to your ability to be of the utmost service in this world. Your commitment to financial freedom is a commitment to the betterment of all beings. When you set yourself free you set others free. You give them permission to break the shackles of "shoulds" and "how-it's-supposed-to-be's" and live a life of their own design. You shine as an example of freedom so that others who see your light of financial well-being can break through their own personal barriers because they see it's possible.

Be the permission to be free. Be the permission to be abundant. Be the permission to not only want what you have, but also to have what you value and to feel the way you want to feel. One more lightbulb ignited makes the whole world brighter. Be that light. Flip the switch. Fall in love with your money. Fall in love with yourself. Fall in love with your life and live the ultimate money love story with happiness and freedom for all.

Appendix

FINANCIAL FREEDOM FREEWAYS

So what are all the different ways to create passive, residual, or recurring income? I'm going to dive into some examples I'm familiar with and go through the positives and negatives of each. Please note that I've not had direct experience with every single one of these Financial Freedom Freeways (FFFs), and I'll make that clear as I discuss each one. This is not a comprehensive list, but it does cover quite a few options.

There are thousands of examples of people all over the world who've created financial freedom using one or more of these avenues, but you need to figure out which is right for you. As you're reading about each FFF, check in with yourself and see what signals your body is giving you. Are you feeling expansive or contracted? Are you feeling excited or freaked out? A little of both, perhaps? This is all incredibly important information to couple with the practical pros and cons I'll outline for each freeway.

You probably won't have an entire business plan mapped out by the end of this section, but there are many more resources to dive into at the back of the book so you can take this concept further. My recommendation is that you start with one FFF and get that rocking and then continue to build multiple streams as you go. If you start off trying to build too many at once you'll lose focus, and perhaps a lot of money. So go through the list here and then determine just one that makes sense for you, your lifestyle, and the amount of capital you currently have to invest.

I'm here as a messenger from the land of financial freedom to say, "Hey! It's possible to live a life spending your time in ways that are meaningful to you and to the world. It's possible for you to leverage your time and be free. Here are some ways to do it and a few tips on getting started."

INTELLECTUAL PROPERTY

Building financial freedom based on your own unique, creative ideas and teachings or products can be a fantastic avenue, especially if you have some sort of specialized skill, knowledge, or way of looking at the world. You can do this in myriad ways, including creating digital products and courses, creating physical products, publishing books, recording albums, or composing and selling songs.

Digital

Examples: My friend Marie Forleo, internet-marketing maven, creates digital products and courses that she sells online in order to leverage herself so that she's not trading hours for dollars. She puts in the work once to create a course or e-book and then she can sell it an infinite number of times. This is a great example of an FFF. (One of her courses, B-School, teaches you how to do the same thing. The link is in the Resources section.)

Pros: You can start a digital empire for free and sell information products as long as you know how to put up a website and format your information properly. Chances are good that you can start this sort of business for less than $500. Anyone can get into this game as long as you have a computer, an internet connection, and something to say, teach, and/or sell. You have ultimate creative freedom on the interwebs and can be whomever you want to be, say whatever you want to say, and run your business how you like because you're not answering to anyone. Plus, you can run your business from anywhere in the world.

Cons: In order for this to work in a long-term, sustainable way, you really do have to have something valuable to say. There are plenty of people creating mediocre information products and selling them online just to make a buck, but they're not doing anyone any favors by doing so. Because there are no barriers to entry, anyone can get online and sell any kind of digital product they like, which is both a pro and a con.

You really need to build a following online in order to do well selling information products. So, you have to learn online marketing skills and be constantly nurturing your audience. To some, this would be a pro, but to those of us who want to be able to step off the grid for a year if we want to, this is a con.

The other issue here is that once someone buys your digital product or course, they have it and they don't need to buy it again. So that means you have to be continually expanding your marketing efforts to find new customers or you have to be continually launching new products to sell to the same customers. For most people hanging out in the digital empire world, this isn't a problem because they're passionate about spreading the word about what they do and creating new content. But, they really aren't financially free unless their living expenses are covered by income that comes in from the sale of their existing products without growing the business any further or making any new products.

Physical Products

Example: I have a friend whose stepfather invented the AirCast, a product used by doctors and hospitals worldwide in orthopedics to help set bones as they heal. AirCast has helped millions of people around the world and is a booming business that my friend has helped grow tremendously. Her stepfather's intellectual property, his invention of the AirCast, has created a business system that brings in revenue whether or not he's actually working in the business anymore, which he is not.

Another example of someone who created financial freedom through using their intellectual property to create a product is my friend Kevin. He created the software program Freehand, and was able to sell it for a huge amount of money.

Pros: If your product hits the market at the right time and is a big hit, there's a lot of money to be made by inventing things and getting them to market. This is a great FFF if you have unique and valuable ideas and have the wherewithal to make them happen.

Cons: You don't ever really know what's going to fly when it gets to market. You may think you have the perfect solution to a problem that you've seen out in the world but then your invention or creation completely flops and you've wasted a lot of time, energy, and resources.

Also, you have to find a really good intellectual property lawyer to make sure that you get well compensated for your creation. Robert Kiyosaki tells a story in his books about how he created the first nylon Velcro surfers' wallet. When it went to market it was a huge hit and they sold thousands of units. Unfortunately, the product wasn't patented or protected in any way and was incredibly easy to duplicate. Pretty soon there were other people on the scene making the same product and Robert went out of business quickly because he didn't have the same resources and distribution to compete with these larger players who were knocking off his original idea. So, if you're selling your ideas, you have to be sure to protect them well.

Books—Traditional Publishing

Examples: I know many authors who've done quite well for themselves by putting their ideas in writing in the form of a book. My mom has written four books, two of which became *New York Times* bestsellers, and I have a few other best-selling friends as well. How it works in the publishing world is that you first need to get an agent who's willing to represent you, then they shop your book around to various publishing houses. When a publishing company decides to take your project on, they sometimes (though not always) give you an advance, which means they're paying you in advance for book sales. Once the book goes on the market, you have to first sell enough books to earn out your advance, and then you can start making royalties. A great deal of my college tuition was paid for through book advances and royalties from my mom's books so I'm quite grateful for this type of income.

People like Stephen King (a fellow Mainer) or Danielle Steel make a substantial living from book advances and royalties because these authors are constantly pumping out new work and they sell a lot of books.

Pros: If you have a computer (or even a typewriter) and an idea, you can write a book. If your book pulls on a particular cultural need or phenomenon at the time and it does really well, you can enjoy the financial rewards of writing a book once and then getting paid over and over again. It doesn't happen to everyone who writes a book, but for those it does happen to, it's a wonderful way to create some residual income. Publishing with a well-known publishing house is also a fantastic way to gain credibility and to benefit from their distribution channels, which most authors wouldn't have access to on their own.

Cons: The idea that if you publish a book with a major publishing company you will automatically become rich and famous is completely erroneous. If you're lucky enough to get a book advance, it may be relatively small and barely enough to cover your living expenses while you write the book (if it even covers that). Many times a book doesn't sell out its advance so the author never receives royalties. The book market is extremely crowded. In the U.S. alone, 328,259 new titles and editions were published in 2010. It really takes a brilliant idea, creative marketing, and great publicity to get a book to become a bestseller. And even then, unless you continue to do speaking engagements and end up on national media, your book won't necessarily continue to sell forever. Earning residuals from publishing a book is not really a passive way of earning income. You have to be out there promoting in order for people to buy the book, so you work for every residual you earn. Lastly, authors earn a very small percentage of every book sold. The publisher takes the largest cut and the author is usually left with about 15 percent, of which they generally give their agent another 15 percent. Most authors are not going to become financially free from writing one book, or even ten. Writing a book takes a lot of work and if you are blessed enough to get picked up by an agent and a great publishing house and even to earn an advance, there are absolutely no guarantees that you'll ever see a royalty check. Lastly, it takes a loooooooong time for a book to go from an idea in your head to a book on a shelf. My mom took four years to write *Women's Bodies, Women's Wisdom* and then there was at least another year and a half of editing, working on cover art, and getting the book to market. The book you're holding in your hands was originally a spark of an idea in May of 2011. We published in September of 2013, so even though it only took me a few months to write, the process is a long one. Be ready to put on your patience pants and have some other ways of bringing in income in the works at the same time because writing a book is definitely not a sure financial bet.

Books—Self-Publishing

Examples: After wading through the list of cons regarding traditional publishing that I just outlined above, many authors choose to go the route of self-publishing for more control over their creative work, a faster turnaround time from writing to publishing, and a larger percentage of the profits. My friend Nancy Levin published her book of poetry called *Writing for My Life* with Balboa Press, Hay House's self-publishing imprint. The whole process from submitting the manuscript to publishing took six weeks, she spent $999 to get the initial package of print and design, and then books are printed on demand. Each book retails for $9.95 and depending on the size of the order she places, she pays $4–$5 each. So far she's made $12,000 on the project. It would have been tricky to find a traditional publisher ready to publish a book of poetry, and then she may have waited forever for the royalties, so Nancy decided to take the bull by the horns and get it done herself. Well done, Nancy!

Another friend of mine, Michael Chase, founder of The Kindness Center, self-published his book in 2009. He started writing it in January of 2009 and had it published and in his hands by July of 2009. Putting the book together cost him nothing besides sweat equity because he did the design himself, and his wife, a professional photographer, took his author photo. He ended up making $4,000 on the book after selling 400 copies because he used a print-on-demand service that charged him $7 to print each book, which sold for $17.95. Great return on investment if you ask me!

The other great part about Michael's story is that his self-published book helped him create a platform (and monetize his existing platform) so that he eventually got a publishing deal. He told me that even though being picked up by a publisher was a dream come true, he's really glad he self-published first because it gave him a much better understanding for the writing and publishing world and for what a publisher actually does.

Pros: As mentioned above, when you opt to self-publish, you get to have creative control over the finished product without a publishing house telling you what you can and can't say and how you can and can't say it. You get full control over the cover design, too. You also get the finished product to market much faster than going the traditional publishing route and you get to keep a significantly higher percentage of the profits. Your only cost is the energy you put into writing the manuscript, perhaps the graphic design for the cover, an editor, and the original cost of printing the book. Other than that, though, when books are sold, you make money right away.

Cons: There are a number of cons in self-publishing. The first, which I also listed as a pro, is that you have complete control, which means that you have to make everything happen. You have to find an editor. You have to find a designer. You have to find a printer. And in order for you to sell a book that's self-published, you have to have a way for people to know about it without the help of a publisher. A large e-mail list, speaking gigs, or some other network to get the word out is a must if you want to sell books. You can't simply put a book up on Amazon and expect people to find it. There's too much clutter in the marketplace. I wouldn't recommend self-publishing unless you have a way to get the word out about your brilliant piece of work. There's also something about being backed by a traditional publishing house that ads to your credibility. Things are changing fast in the publishing world, but as I write this, Random House, Penguin, Simon & Schuster, Hay House, and more are still standing and producing wonderful work. When you self-publish you don't have access to the clout or distribution network of a large publishing house, which can put you at a disadvantage.

There's almost no limit to the type of intellectual property you can create a business around. Simply know what you're getting yourself into, make sure you get the protection you need, and don't put all of your eggs in one basket. Enjoy the creative process and the gift of being able to get your work into the world. Make sure you're being smart about the business end or that you have someone on your team who can help you with that part.

INVESTING

Examples: You can invest in paper assets like stocks and bonds, real estate, or businesses to get your money to work for you instead of you working for your money. My dear friend Barbara Stanny, one of my biggest mentors, earns most of her money because she's been a smart investor. She earns significant passive income from the interest, dividends, and other income from the money she's invested in real estate, bonds, and the stock market, and she does quite well.

Robert Kiyosaki made most of his initial fortune in the real estate industry in Phoenix in the '90s. He and his wife would buy a property, get it ready for renting, then rent it out for more than they were spending on the mortgage and maintenance and enjoy the positive cash flow, or passive investment income. As their business grew they invested in larger residential properties and in commercial properties. When they first became financially free they lived entirely from their real estate income and they didn't have to work. In fact, Kiyosaki forced himself to take an entire year off.

You can also invest in businesses. Venture capitalists make their money this way. When someone has a business idea that you believe in, you can give them a chunk of money in exchange for part ownership in the company. You may be a silent partner, who doesn't weigh in on the business and is just investing money, or you may become an advisor and invest both money and insight to help the company grow. Then, when/if the company begins to turn a large profit and get bigger, you have a stake in the company that is worth a lot more than the money you initially invested. Sean Parker, the guy who created Napster, invested in Facebook when it was just a wee babe. As Facebook grew to the monolith it is now, his stake in the company grew and he is now worth billions as a result. When you invest in a company you can either be a venture capitalist and get part ownership in a company or an angel investor who simply puts money into start-ups and doesn't get ownership in the company, but does get an agreement that when/if the company grows they'll get a return on their investment and their money will grow.

Pros: Investing is a great way to grow money that you already have. You can put your money somewhere like a stock or in real estate or in a start-up, and then wait for it to grow as the market improves or as the company grows. It's also a fantastic way to vote for what you value and believe in with your dollars. For example, if you value sustainability and social consciousness, you can put your money in companies that operate according to those values and help expand what they're doing to make a bigger impact on the planet.

Cons: Investing is one of the places where the old adage "It takes money to make money" is simply true. You need investment capital to invest. And if you don't know what you're doing, it's easy to lose money. If you don't know the real estate market where you're investing in rental properties, it's easy for those investments to go south and for you to start losing money fast. Also, though each person makes up the economy and we can all do our small part to direct it where we'd like to see it go, we have no control over the overall market. So, if you had all of your money invested in the stock market in 2008 during the credit crash, you lost a lot of money and there was nothing that you could do about it. Many wise financial advisors I've learned from say to only put money in the stock market that you could stand to lose every penny of. Investing is a higher-stakes game so I would recommend working with a professional whom you trust when it comes to paper assets, and really doing your research when it comes to real estate and investing in businesses. Know that it's risky and just decide how much risk you're comfortable with and how much you would be comfortable losing before you start writing checks.

TRADITIONAL BIG BUSINESS

Example: People who own large companies that have a system that works whether they're physically present or not are another great example. Whether Bill Gates shows up at work or not, Microsoft is still bringing in money and Bill Gates is still making a whole bunch of it. (Though I'm sure he shows up a lot and gives his heart and soul to his company because he chooses to. Key word: *chooses*.) Most people who start a traditional business such as a restaurant or a retail store end up being stuck in self-employed land where if they don't show up, nothing happens. Some, however, figure out a way to make themselves dispensable and hire great people to run their company so that they can go off and do whatever they want. They value freedom more than feeling important and needed. There's also an important difference here to point out between working in your company because you have to in order for revenue to be generated and working in your company because you love it. Blake Mycoskie, founder of TOMS shoes and author of *Start Something That Matters*, focuses primarily on speaking and giving away shoes. He has other people run the day-to-day matters of his company because he loves and prefers the outreach part. He's free because he can choose to spend his time on the things he loves to do. But TOMS shoes does not need Blake in there working on stuff every single day for revenue to be generated. He has a system that pays him whether he shows up or not.

Pros: A traditional business that grows large enough to generate revenue whether you show up or not is a wonderful thing to have. Being a B-quadrant business owner gives you the freedom to create a product that you believe in and to run the company the way you want to, just like Blake Mycoskie. No one else was running a for-profit company where they just gave away one of their product for each one sold, but because Blake was the founder and owner he could create a business model that spoke to him, and he did just that with pairs of shoes. When you run your own business you don't have to do it like anyone tells you to. You get to call the shots. And then when you hire amazing people to run your company for you, you get to enjoy working on the parts of it that you love and that you're best at and leave the rest to someone else while continuing to reap the benefits of the work you put in setting up the system in the first place.

Cons: Ninety-five percent of all businesses fail within the first five years, so there's nothing about going into business that guarantees success. And, as I mentioned before, most people who start their own company, regardless of what industry they're in, never make it out of the S-quadrant where money making is totally dependent on them showing up to make the doughnuts. Finding great people to run your company can be tough, and letting go of control when you do find great people can be even tougher. Creating a successful big business also takes a lot of time, energy, resources, and creativity. You have to create the product, the manufacturing, the distribution, marketing, customer service, research and development, and every other aspect that makes a company run. It's all starting from the ground up without a system of success to follow. Starting a company that you will eventually grow big enough to either have other people run or that you'll sell for a large sum is not for the faint of heart. My recommendation would be to do it only if you have such a burning passion that nothing else will satisfy you. My sister Ann told me a story of a famous actor who taught a master class to the theater department at Yale. During his talk he told them, "If there's anything else on earth that you would be as happy doing as you would be acting, do that instead." That's pretty much how I feel about starting a traditional business.

FRANCHISING

Example: A franchise is when a large company creates a system that other people (franchisees) can purchase and run. The franchisee doesn't have to create the product or the business system. They just have to invest in getting it off the ground in their own community. McDonald's is a franchise and so is Panera Bread. I have a friend from childhood whose dad owns several McDonald's restaurants around southern Maine where we grew up. He seemed to have quite a bit of freedom because he had managers for all of his locations so he didn't have to physically show up for Big Macs to be sold.

Pros: When you purchase a franchise you get a business model that's pre-done for you so it doesn't take as much energy as starting a traditional business. The product has been created already. The marketing has been created. The business model is established. All you have to do is plug people, resources, and energy into the system to get it going. This is a great model for someone who wants to capitalize on a business that's already been proven.

Cons: Most franchises cost upward of $100,000 to purchase, and some of the larger ones like McDonald's can be over $1 million to start. So this is not the way to go unless you have a lot of start-up capital to invest. Also, even though there's a business system that you follow, there's no guarantee that it will work in your town, and you have to pay the franchisor whether you're making money or not. It's hard to find good staff, especially to work at a fast-food restaurant, which many franchises are. Having constant employee turnover is exhausting, and many bosses call their companies "adult daycare" because of the headaches of having staff. Lastly, many franchises produce a product that would be hard to stand behind, even if it makes good money. For example, do you really want to make your money selling fast food and contributing to the obesity epidemic, diabetes, and heart disease? Here's my two cents: if you're going to go the route of franchising, at least choose one that's doing a service to the planet like Curves, a gym for women, or Chipotle, a Mexican fast-food restaurant that has organic, grass-fed meats and uses recycled materials.

NETWORK MARKETING

Example: And then there's the industry that I got my start in, network marketing. This is where a company who manufactures a product or creates a service distributes it through word of mouth and pays the consumer to spread the word. It's like a mini-franchise because there's already a product and system in place for you. You just have to spread the word.

I started my network marketing business when I was 18 years old for less than $700. Starting with my parents' friends and my friends' parents, and then eventually expanding beyond that network, I began to organically spread the word about the products that I used and loved. I was proudly representing them and sharing how they could help the people in my life. By the end of college I had created enough residual income through my customers and my team of distributors who I'd enrolled that I was able to graduate from Brown and not get a "real job." (My income at that time was about $40,000 annually.) When I did decide to get a real job in NYC just to prove to myself that I could, I lasted about four months until the event planning company I worked for asked me to cancel all of my weekend plans at the last minute to help throw a party for an important client of theirs. I refused to let someone else own my time like that so, soon after that weekend, I quit and put all my efforts toward building my network marketing business.

My aunt and uncle, Penny and Phil Kirk, are some of the top income earners with the company my family and I partner with, USANA Health Sciences. Since 1994, the year they joined USANA, they've steadily grown their customer and distributor base. Every week Penny and Phil earn a commission from the health products sold in their organization, whether they're climbing to Mt. Everest base camp, which they did with my grandmother a few years ago, or hanging out with friends in the south of France. Penny and Phil have traveled the world and lived in more than 28 homes in their 40 years of marriage. They are the ultimate freedom-loving vagabonds, but instead of being nomadic while struggling financially, like most people, they get to do it while enjoying total financial freedom. They've also been able to support the music careers of their three sons through the residual income of their USANA business, which brings them tremendous joy.

Pros: Anyone can start a network marketing business. There are no limitations in terms of age, gender, education, or experience. If you have a willingness to learn and go beyond your comfort zone, you can do it. There's a very low start-up cost and you have a virtual business in network marketing so there's very little monthly overhead, if any. There's virtually no risk because most companies require an initial investment of less than $1,000 and for that you get the products that the company makes to enjoy with your family. You get to plug in to a proven system with training and support provided for you, most often for no additional cost. There's a product that's already been created, a research and development department, a customer service center, a returns processing center, a manufacturing facility, and a shipping department, not to mention the corporate team. All these people are in place to help you build your business but you're not responsible for paying their salaries, training them, hiring them, or firing them. Running a network marketing business will teach you the business skills you need to succeed in any venture you may pursue for the rest of your life: communication skills, presenting skills, public speaking, time management, organization, marketing, sales skills, and personal growth. Warren Buffet, Donald Trump, and Richard Branson all own or are stakeholders in network marketing companies. Robert Kiyosaki recommends that anyone who wants to learn about business and residual income spend five years with a good network marketing company simply for the training and skills they'll receive, regardless of the income they'll create. I can personally attest to this as every skill I've used to become successful with my online business, as a public speaker, workshop facilitator, and overall businesswoman has come from running my network marketing business. If you want to be successful in anything in life, you're going to have to learn sales skills and there's nothing like network marketing to teach you this, especially with a team that does it in a totally non-sleazy, heart-centered way like my team.

Cons: Building a successful network marketing business requires you to get out of your own way and challenge any limiting beliefs you may have about marketing or sales. It requires you to get over your fear of rejection (which you may as well get over sooner rather than later in life because a little rejection is inevitable if you're building anything worthwhile). It requires getting out of your comfort zone, which is something that many people are simply not willing to do. You also really need to be a people person to be successful in network marketing. You have to love meeting and connecting with new people on a regular basis. (You don't have to be an extrovert, you just have to like people.)

There are certain unprofessional practices used in some network marketing companies that give the entire industry a bad name. My team and I have coined the term "conscious network marketing" because we're out to change the way the entire industry is perceived. This means that we don't try to convince anyone to do anything, we're never trying to get someone to buy something or sign up for something that they don't want to buy or sign up for, and that our businesses are heart-centered and based on service.

Any business worth anything has at its core the desire to make people's lives better. The truth is that if you focus on service and adding value to the world, you're on the right track. But focusing on those things without thinking about your business model and how you can eventually work yourself out of the system so that you can focus only on the things that you love doing is a mistake that many people make. Then 20 years down the line they look up from their desk with bloodshot eyes and can't remember why they started in the first place. They're so burned-out that they can't even remember who they are, let alone what they love to do.

Don't let this be your fate. Pick one of the FFFs described and begin to incorporate it as one stream of income in your life. If you currently are an employee, great! Stick with that and then carve out some time on the side to start something else to build toward financial freedom for yourself, like a network marketing business. This does not have to happen overnight so please be patient with yourself. If it takes 10 or even 15 years to create enough recurring income to cover your living expenses for the rest of your life to allow you to do whatever you want, wouldn't that be worth it? You're not going to create that working for someone else, so you might as well start something on the side. Pick the thing that resonates with you the most and get going.

RESOURCES

Here are some other resources available to you as you continue on the Money Love journey. I've read all of these books, visited these sites, and personally taken all of these programs. They've all worked wonders in my own financial life, and I know they'll do the same for you.

And, don't forget to visit www.moneyalovestory.com to continue the journey with me and the other people who are working and playing with this material. I'll be updating the resources there on an ongoing basis so check back often and be sure to subscribe for updates.

BOOKS

The $100 Startup by Chris Guillebeau

The 4-Hour Workweek by Timothy Ferriss

The 9 Steps to Financial Freedom by Suze Orman

Ask and It Is Given by Jerry and Esther Hicks

The Dynamic Laws of Prosperity by Catherine Ponder

The Education of Millionaires by Michael Ellsberg

The Fire Starter Sessions by Danielle LaPorte

The Game of Life and How to Play It by Florence Scovel Shinn

Overcoming Underearning by Barbara Stanny

Prince Charming Isn't Coming: How Women Get Smart About Money by Barbara Stanny

Rich Dad, Poor Dad by Robert Kiyosaki

Secrets of Six-Figure Women by Barbara Stanny

Smart Women Finish Rich by David Bach

The Tapping Solution by Nick Ortner

Think and Grow Rich by Napoleon Hill

WEBSITES

www.dailyworth.com

www.mint.com

www.debtorsanonymous.org

www.underearnersanonymous.org

www.moneyalovestory.com

MY PROGRAMS

The Freedom Family—Our network marketing community within USANA: www.thefreedomfam.com

Other programs: www.katenorthrup.com/shop

OTHER PROGRAMS

Marie Forleo's B-School: www.moneyalovestory.com/bschool

The Desire Map by Danielle LaPorte: www.moneyalovestory.com/desire

Money Clarity by Daily Worth: www.moneyalovestory.com/moneyclarity

ACKNOWLEDGMENTS

As I was reading through this book one last time before sending it off to print, it struck me that it's not really mine. My name may be on the cover, but this book contains the work, hearts, souls, and stories of thousands. And for that I'm beyond grateful.

I stand on the shoulders of giants. I feel incredibly blessed to have been born at this time to walk a path prepaved by the footsteps of those who've come before me. Thank you to all the way-showers, women and men who dared to suggest a new perspective, and for everyone who's ever chosen to do something differently than everyone else.

There's no way these pages could contain the depth of my gratitude for all the help and inspiration I've had along the way, but I shall do what I can to scratch the surface.

This book began as a tiny seed when I started teaching "Women and Wealth" seminars with **Maggie Pierce**. Without your desire to co-create and teach women a new financial perspective, none of this would have happened. Thank you.

A special thank you to **Nancy Reid**, as well for rocking "Women and Wealth" with me so many times in NYC. We sure were a dynamic duo.

Thank you to everyone in **Team Northrup** and **The Freedom Family** who continues to spread the message of financial freedom and vibrant health around the world. Our business family makes my heart burst with love and pride.

Barbara Stanny, thank you for inspiring me to finally get it together financially. Your boundless tough love and your "Overcoming Underearning" seminar are what turned it around for me.

Janice Goldman Pickler, for being my first financial advisor and for making it safe to admit that I didn't have it all together.

Danielle LaPorte, when you told me, "YOU are the opportunity," everything changed. Thank you for stoking the fire that eventually set me free. And thank you for being the kind of friend who flies across the country to celebrate.

Regena Thomashauer, **Nicole Daedone**, and **Dame Lori Sutherland**, you ladies gave me permission to have fun and pleasure with my money. And it's been revolutionary.

Patty Gift, your last name says it all. You sat next to me during my workshop at the Reveal Conference and then asked if I wanted to write a book. Your "seeing me," your friendship, and your guidance mean the world to me. Also, thanks for being a damn good editor.

Laura Gray, you took my ideas and helped them make sense. Thank you for thinking so differently than me and for working your editorial magic on these pages.

Thank you to **Chris Guillebeau**. Your *Art of Non-Conformity* book event in Portland, Maine, inspired The Freedom Tour. And I am forever grateful for the introduction to **David Fugate**, my delightful, easy-to-work-with agent, who believed in my work in a moment when it really needed believing in.

I took a class at Brown called "Entrepreneurship and Good Work" that answered the question, "Is it possible to make good money, do meaningful work, and be happy all at the same time?" That class changed my life. Thank you **Professor Josef Mittlemann** for asking and answering questions that really matter and for proving to me that money, service, and happiness can all coexist beautifully.

To the **Northrup clan**: Granny, Anne, Rachel, Karl, Jill, Jake, Jen, John, Annie, Billy, Lori, Jacob, Nigel, Matt, Ebony, and Grandad, for marching to the beat of your own drums in business and in life. I'm grateful to share "out of the box" genes with you all.

Penny and Phil Kirk, thank you for fanning the flames of my 14-year-old entrepreneurial spirit. Thank you for being mentors in matters of business, spirituality, and life. Your guidance continues to be invaluable.

To **Kris Carr** and the **Crazy Sexy Women**, you know who you are: our posse of love and support wows me on a weekly basis.

Kirsten Lewis, Heather Graham, Moby, and **Annie Moller**: all hail The Witches of Norton. Thank you for all of the magic.

Thank you **Dr. Mryon Wentz** for your vision and to everyone at **USANA Health Sciences**, including **Dave Wentz** and **Dan Macuga**, for building and maintaining a beautiful, integral vehicle for freedom for thousands, including me. **Lori Truman**, thank you especially for your leadership and love.

Dyana Valentine, you wacky, wonderful woman: thank you for being the first person to read this book and shower her with your love and brilliance. And thank you for showering me with the same.

Cheryl Richardson, thank you for your seemingly random suggestion that I attend Movers and Shakers. **Reid Tracy**, thanks for publishing my book. **Louise Hay**, for starting it all. **Mollie Langer**, thanks for bringing us all together. **Nancy Levin**, for shining your light so brightly that the whole world can see a little bit better.

Meggan Watterson, for being my lady love soul sister and for giving me and women around the world permission to reveal ourselves.

Rebecca Bent and the **Handel Group** for seeing my potential long before I caught even a glimmer of it.

Colleen Saidman, Rodney Yee, and **Josh Pais**: thank you for teaching me to tell the truth.

Chela Davison, for helping me take my seat.

Ned Leavitt and **Gail Larsen**, thank you for hearing my voice in two very different, but equally critical ways.

Marie Forleo, thank you for being a new model of prosperity and for being a kick-ass mentor and friend.

To **Noah Levy, Ellen Folan, Raina Rahbar, Carissa Reiniger, Michelle Phillips, Michael Chase, Andrea Coles, Laura Garnett, Nisha Moodley, Rochelle Schieck, Deborah Kern, Liza Pascal, Ayan Rivera, Jill Rogers, Kelly Turner, Aaron Teich, Melanie Ericksen, Mike Perry, Hope Matthews, Lucas Foglia, Sasha Rubel, Sandra Chiu, Terri Cole, Jessica Ortner, Rachel Goldstein, Jessica Shepard, KC Baker, Liz Dialto, James Wedmore, Alisa Vitti, Liz Rider, Gabrielle Bernstein, Latham Thomas**, and my dear **Danielle Vieth**: your friendship, support, humor, and love floated me through this process. Thank you for your advice, for letting me practice on you, for sending me love notes, for calling me, for asking great questions, and mostly just for being there.

Thank you to everyone who hosted Mike and me on **The Freedom Tour.** Your open arms and homes made it possible.

To the **Yarmouth Girls** (Ellen, Emma, Lindsay, Hannah, Morgan, Meghan, Liz, and Rebecca) for being there right from the beginning. Your friendship means more than you know.

To **Bill and Michele Watts** for raising one heck of a great man.

Diane Grover, you are one of the most impressive women I know. Thank you for maintaining the sacred order for so many years. And **Charlie,** thanks for taking such great care of Di so she can take such great care of everyone else.

Tracey Moller, thank you for your enthusiasm for this project and for your love. I feel blessed to have you in my life. And **Waverly,** thanks for giving me the chance to be a big sister. I couldn't have asked for a more perfect little sister than you.

To **Ann Moller,** my sister, my best friend, and my pinch-hitter editor: thank you for the giggles, for your way with words, for your belief in me, and for your love. I am blessed indeed.

Dad, thanks for being there no matter what, even through the bumpy stuff. Thanks for passing down your love for and skill with the English language. And thanks for being the perfect dad for me.

Mom, for your legacy, your love, and for a first chakra the size of Texas. Thank you for never being like the other mothers. I couldn't be more grateful that we chose one another this time around.

To **Mike**, thanks for being my man, for driving this road with me, for all the adventures we've had, and for all of the ones that are still to come. And most of all, for loving me and letting me love you.

For those of you in my community online whether it be KateNorthrup.com, Facebook, Twitter, or Instagram, thanks for playing and for taking this #MoneyLove journey together.

And a deep bow to YOU. Thank you, dear reader, for being here with me. Without you none of this could be.